Commercial Hydroponics

Commercial Hydroponics

John Mason

Kangaroo Press

Acknowledgments

This book is the culmination of many years of personal observation and experience, both my own and from many others who have so generously given their advice and comments. In particular we wish to thank the following people and organisations:

Keith Maxwell, Australian ISOSC representative and hydroponics consultant
Rick Donnan, Growool Australia, Sydney
Robert Van Aurich, Aquaponics, Perth, WA
Joe Romer, R & D Chemicals, Sydney NSW
Greg Seymour, Dept Agriculture, NSW
Brian Hearne, Simple Grow, Sydney, NSW
Carol and Frank Griesser of Hydrofresh Produce, Wedderburn
Gary Andrews, Growing Systems Australia, Melbourne
Mike Hartley, CSR Australia
Ray Wadsworth, Australian Perlite, Sydney
Students and staff of the Australian Horticultural Correspondence School

Contributors
Sections of the book were written by:

Iain Harrison, Senior Tutor with the Australian Horticultural Correspondence School
Alison Bundock, Tutor with the Australian Horticultural Correspondence School
Keith Maxwell, hydroponics consultant, Sydney, Australia

Research
Iain Harrison and Alison Bundock

Drawings
Peter Mason and John Mason

Photography
John Mason and Leonie Mason
with contributions from: Keith Maxwell, Robert Van Aurich, Rick Donnan, Carol and Frank Griesser

Thanks to Paul Colcheedas for photos taken at Eliza Bottoms Nursery

Reprinted in 1992
First published in 1990 by Kangaroo Press Pty Ltd
3 Whitehall Road (P.O. Box 75) Kenthurst NSW 2156
Typeset by Midland Typesetters Pty Ltd
Printed in Hong Kong through Colorcraft Ltd

ISBN 0 86417 300 8

Contents

Foreword

This is a book for practising hydroponic growers. It is not a scientific text.

The intention is to provide a book which is easy to read and readily understood by anyone wanting to grow plants hydroponically. The reader does not need to have a scientific background to understand it. A certain amount of scientific understanding is required by anyone growing plants hydroponically though, and that necessary understanding is developed through the early chapters of this book in a way which can be readily grasped by the lay person.

Part 1

1 Introduction

Hydroponics is the technique of growing plants without soil.

The roots grow either in air, which is kept very humid; in water, which is well aerated; or in some solid, non-soil medium, which is kept moist. The water around the roots contains a carefully balanced mixture of nutrients which provides food for the plant.

There are three main ways of growing plants hydroponically:

Aggregate culture
Small particles of chemically inert substances provide a suitable environment for the plant roots to grow in.

Rockwool culture
A fibrous sponge-like material made from molten rock provides an environment for the roots to grow through.

Water culture
Water, perhaps mixed with air (with no solid material), provides the environment in which the roots grow.

The aggregate, rockwool or water which is used to provide the root environment, supplies the physical needs of the roots.

The roots (and in fact the whole plant) also have chemical needs which must be catered to. The chemical needs are supplied by adding a carefully calculated solution of nutrients to the root zone, and maintaining the balance of chemicals in that solution at appropriate levels.

Hydroponics has also been called 'soilless culture', 'nutriculture' and 'chemiculture'.

History

The word hydroponics comes from two Greek words: 'hydro' meaning water and 'ponos' meaning labour. This word was first used by Dr W. F. Gericke, a Californian professor who in 1929 began to develop what had previously been a laboratory technique into a commercial means of growing plants. Throughout the 19th century a number of scientists undertook significant research into the nature of plant nutrition. Classical experiments conducted by German plant scientists, Sachs in 1860 and Knop between 1861 and 1865, led to our first understanding of what were essential plant nutrients. Chemical formulae developed by Sachs and Knop, and several other researchers who followed them, provided Dr Gericke with the knowledge to make an effective nutrient solution, thus overcoming the major restriction to the development of hydroponic culture.

Plants had been grown hydroponically before Dr Gericke, but only as laboratory experiments or (in the case of some earlier civilisations), without a proper understanding of the methods being used. Dr Gericke is credited with having recognised the commercial potential of what he had seen as a laboratory technique, and having conducted trials which inspired the development of a commercial industry in the following decades.

Scientists in North America, Europe and Japan, inspired by Dr Gericke's experiences, worked throughout the 1930s and 40s to refine our knowledge of hydroponic growing. The United States army used hydroponic culture to grow fresh food for troops stationed on infertile Pacific islands during World War II. By the 1950s there were viable commercial hydroponic farms operating in America, Britain, Europe, Africa and Asia.

Interest in hydroponics developed in Australia throughout the 1960s, and in the 1970s many vegetable growers, inspired by tales of increased production, attempted to convert their operations to hydroponics. Unfortunately, many of these people failed to do their 'homework', and embarked upon schemes without having a real understanding of the differences between soil and hydroponic culture. The result was many failures, and the development of an attitude in Australia that hydroponics doesn't really work.

In 1981 CSR Ltd established an Australian plant to produce horticultural grade rockwool for hydroponic production. CSR did their homework, promoted their product well and supported it with excellent technical information. As a result, Growool (as it is known) became widely accepted, and today is used extensively in the Australian cut flower industry. Australian vegetable growers have continued to be slow in adopting hydroponics, perhaps due to bad experiences in the 1970s.

At the beginning of the 1990s commercial crops of vegetables, berry fruit and cut flowers are grown extensively by hydroponic culture in many countries. The most popular technique worldwide would be rockwool culture, though NFT (Nutrient Film Technique), perlite and gravel bed culture are all very significant techniques in use in commercial hydroponics.

How Plants Grow

To understand and practise hydroponics successfully requires the grower to have an understanding of how plants grow.

Almost all plants grown in hydroponics are flowering plants. These plants have four main parts:

Roots—the parts which grow below the soil
Stems—the framework
Leaves—required for respiration, transpiration and photosynthesis
Reproductive parts—flowers and fruits.

Roots

Soil provides the plant with the following:

• Nutrients • Water • Air • Support

Roots absorb nutrients, water and gases, transmitting these 'chemicals' to feed other parts of the plant. Roots hold the plant in position and stop it from falling over or blowing away.

When we grow a plant in hydroponics we must make sure that nutrients, water and air are still supplied and that the plant is supported, as would occur if it was growing in soil.

Nutrient supply in soil is a more complex matter than in hydroponics. Plant nutrients can be supplied, broadly speaking, in three different forms:

Water soluble simple chemical compounds
Nutrients in these compounds are readily available to plants (i.e. the plant can absorb them quickly and easily).

Less soluble simple chemical compounds
The nutrients in these compounds can be used by plants without needing to undergo any chemical change, but because they don't dissolve so easily in water they aren't as readily usable as the more soluble compounds. The diminished solubility may be because of the nature of the compound (e.g. superphosphate) or may be due to something else (e.g. slow release fertilisers such as Osmocote, which is made by incorporating the simple chemicals inside a semi-permeable bubble—thus nutrients move slowly out of the bubble).

This second group of nutrients, when placed in soil, will last longer than the first group of water soluble nutrients.

Complex chemical compounds
These require chemical changes to occur before the nutrients can be absorbed by plants. They include organic manures and fertilisers which need to be broken down by soil microorganisms into a form which the plant can use. They also include other complex fertilisers which need to be affected by natural acids in the soil, or heat from the sun, to become simple compounds which the plant roots can use.

Complex chemicals release their nutrients gradually over a long period of time, depending on the range of chemical changes needed to take place before the plant can use them.

Plants grown in a soil derive their nutrients from all three types of compounds. The availability of these compounds varies not only according to the group they come from but also with factors such as heat, water, soil acids and microorganisms present. Consequently, it is impossible to control the availability of nutrients in soil.

This is one intrinsic advantage of hydroponics over soil growing. In hydroponics you can choose to use only simple, soluble compounds, and so you can determine the exact amount of each essential nutrient available to a plant at any point in time.

Stems

The main stem and its branches are the framework that support the leaves, flowers and fruits. The leaves, and also green stems, manufacture food by the process known as photosynthesis, and this is transported to the flowers, fruits and roots. The vascular system within the stem consists of canals, or vessels, which transfer nutrients and water upwards and downwards through the plant. This is equivalent to the blood system in animals.

Leaves

The primary function of leaves is photosynthesis, a process in which light energy is caught from the sun and stored via a chemical reaction in the form of carbohydrates such as sugars. The energy can then be retrieved and used at a later date if required in a process known as respiration. Leaves are also the principle plant part involved in the process known as transpiration whereby water evaporating, mainly through the leaf pores (or stomata), sometimes through the leaf cuticle (or surface) as well, passes out of the leaf into a drier external environment. This evaporating water helps regulate the temperature of the plant. This process may also operate in the reverse direction whereby water vapour from a humid external environment will pass into the drier leaf.

The process of water evaporating from the leaves is very important in that it creates a water gradient or potential between the upper and lower parts of the plant. As the water evaporates from the plant cells in the leaves then more water is drawn from neighbouring cells to replace the lost water. Water is then drawn into those neighbouring cells from their neighbours and from conducting vessels in the stems. This process continues, eventually drawing water into the roots from the ground until the water gradient has been sufficiently reduced. As the water moves throughout the plant it carries nutrients, hormones, enzymes, etc. In effect this

passage of water through the plant has a similar effect to a water pump, in this case causing water to be drawn from the ground, through the plant and eventually out into the atmosphere.

Reproductive parts

Almost all plants grown in hydroponics are flowering plants. These reproduce by pollen (i.e. male parts) fertilising an egg (i.e. female part found in the ovary of a flower). The ovary then grows to produce a fruit and the fertilised egg(s) grow to produce seed.

There can sometimes be difficulty in obtaining a good crop because insufficient pollen reaches the female parts, resulting in insufficient fruit forming. (This will be discussed in Chapter 11.)

Classification of Hydroponic Systems

There are two main groups of systems:

• *Water culture*
Nutrients are dissolved in water which is brought in contact with the roots.
Water is either aerated or roots are allowed to contact air as well as nutrient solution.
Trellis, wire mesh or some other support is provided above the nutrient solution

Examples:
Nutrient tank
Standard jar
Nutrient film (NFT)
Mist systems

• *Aggregate culture*
Nutrients are dissolved in water which is moved into the root area.
The roots are grown in solid material (inert—free of nutrient) which is chosen to hold sufficient moisture but drain off the excess, allowing adequate aeration.
The solid material which the roots grow in contributes towards (if not fully supplying) anchorage.

Examples:
Beds, tier systems etc.

The Variables of a System

The types of hydroponic system that can be used vary for a variety of reasons. The most common variables are:

1. Solution dispensation
—closed or open (i.e. is the solution recycled or drained through and lost)
—drip, slop, capillary feed, wicks, misting, dry fertilising etc.
2. Automatic or manual operation
3. Type of medium
—gravel, vermiculite, perlite, sand, scoria, peat, expanded clay, a mixture etc.
4. Construction materials
—concrete, fibreglass, plastic, glass, wood, masonry, metal, PVC, ceramic, polystyrene etc. What will your container be?
5. Rate and frequency of irrigation and feeding
6. Air injection (in water culture, where air is pumped into nutrient solution to raise the oxygen level)
7. Plant support
—trellis etc.
8. Environmental controls
—temperature, ventilation etc.

Overview of the Industry

Worldwide, the interest in commercial hydroponics has steadily increased over the past few decades. Hydroponic growing is certainly significant in market gardening, but more so in some countries than others.

There would certainly be more than 5000 hectares of commercial hydroponic production worldwide. This compares with around 100 hectares in 1960. Total production area in some countries, particularly many eastern bloc countries, is not known.

Unsuccessful attempts at hydroponics in the US, Australia and some other countries during the early years contributed towards a bad reputation for this type of production. This impeded development of commercial installations in those countries. Other countries, such as the UK and the Netherlands, which were more successful with their early attempts, found it easier to develop a viable hydroponic industry.

The Netherlands accounts for more than 50% of the known area under production. The UK accounts for more than 10%. No other country accounts for much more than 5%. Australia's hydroponic industry is estimated at just under 100 hectares, but growing steadily.

On an international basis, rockwool is the most commonly used system by far, with NFT or aggregate culture being particularly significant in some countries.

Why Practise Hydroponics?

Hydroponics has been practised by market gardeners and other growers since the 1940s. The advantages of hydroponics are many; however, the disadvantages should not be overlooked when you are deciding whether or not to set up a hydroponics system.

Advantages

1. You can grow anywhere
Crops can be grown where no suitable soil exists or where the soil is contaminated with disease.

2. Culture is intensive
A lot can be grown in a small space, over a short period of time. It is also possible to grow in multi-levels. Where transportation costs to the market are significant (e.g. in the centre of large cities), hydroponic farms may be viable irrespective of land values.
Example: In Japan, vegetables are grown in supermarkets in the centre of large cities. The savings on transport costs and the benefit of having fresh produce offsets the increased cost of space in these cities.

3. Heavy work is reduced
Labour for tilling the soil, cultivation, fumigation, watering and other traditional practices can be reduced and sometimes eliminated.

4. Water is conserved
A well designed, properly run hydroponic system uses less water than soil gardening.

5. Pest and disease problems are reduced
The need to fumigate is lessened. Soil-borne plant diseases are more easily eradicated in many nutriculture systems. This is particularly true in 'closed systems' which can be totally flooded with an eradicant. The chance of soil-borne human

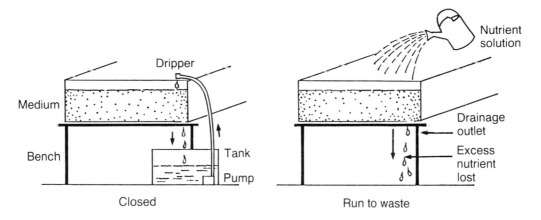

Simple aggregate-bed hydroponic systems. The system on the left has recirculating (closed) method of solution dispensation. After being applied to the top of the bed, any excess nutrient solution drains through the aggregate and is collected in the container (or tank) below. From there a pump is used periodically to return solution to the top of the bed. The system on the right has an open (also called 'run to waste') method of solution dispensation. Any excess solution runs through the aggregate, out of the drainage hole and is lost.

disease is also reduced. Though rare in developed countries, it is possible for diseases to be transmitted from animal manures or soil microorganisms onto food plants grown in soil, leading to illness.

6. Weed problems are almost eliminated

7. Yields can be maximised
Maximum yields are possible, making the system economically feasible in high density and expensive land areas.

8. Nutrients are conserved
This can lead to a reduction in pollution of land and streams because valuable chemicals needn't be lost.

9. The environment is more easily controlled
For example, in greenhouse type operations the light, temperature, humidity and composition of the atmosphere can be manipulated, while in the root zone the timing and frequency of nutrient feeding and irrigation can be readily controlled.

10. Root zone chemistry is easier to control
Salt toxicities can be leached out; pH can be adjusted; EC (electroconductivity) can be adjusted. Also salts will not bind chemically to the majority of media used in hydroponics so problems of salt buildup that may occur in soils, particularly when highly soluble nutrients are used, are uncommon in hydroponics.

11. New plants are easier to establish
Transplant shock is reduced.

12. Crop rotation/fallowing is not necessary
All areas can be used at all times—you don't need to leave a paddock for a year to fallow every so often.

The amateur horticulturist can use hydroponic systems in the home, even in high rise buildings. A nutriculture system can be clean, light weight and mechanised.

Disadvantages

1. Initial cost is high
The original construction cost per hectare is great. This may limit you to growing crops which either turn over fast or give a high return.

2. Skill and knowledge are needed to operate properly
Trained plantsmen must direct the growing operation. Knowledge of how plants grow and the principles of nutrition are important.

3. Diseases and pests can spread quickly through a system
Introduced diseases and nematodes may be quickly spread to all beds using the same nutrient tank in a closed system.

4. Beneficial soil life is normally absent

5. Plants react fast to both good and bad conditions
The plants in hydroponics react more quickly to changes in growing conditions. This means that the hydroponic gardener needs to watch his plants more closely for changes.

6. Available plant varieties are not always ideal
Most available plant varieties have been developed for growth in soil and in the open. Development of varieties which are specifically adapted to more controlled conditions may be slow to occur.

2 Site Considerations

What you can grow successfully in a hydroponic installation is largely dependent upon where you are located. The local climate, availability and quality of water and local demand for what is grown are all key considerations.

Climate

Climate affects what can be grown, and at what times of the year it can be grown. Even with the help of greenhouses or other environmental controls, the outside environment still has a great bearing upon the economic viability of using hydroponic systems.

It is not simply a matter of the quality of the environment, quantity is also critical (e.g. to grow cucumbers it is not just enough to just get warm weather, the number of days of warm weather is also critical).

Some of the more important factors to consider are:

Temperature

Temperature affects the development of flowers or fruit in many different types of plants. Very often the plant not only needs the temperature to be at a certain level, but it needs the right sequence of day temperatures (e.g. many chrysanthemums need a sequence where day temperatures are warm during the early stages of flower development but gradually become cooler as the flower buds develop and approach maturity).

Frost Sensitive Period

Frost can kill or severely damage a crop. Bad frosts will to some extent even penetrate the walls of a greenhouse, burning plants inside. Even plants which are generally tolerant of frosts can be badly affected if the frost occurs at the wrong time of year:

- Virtually all fruit or flower buds are susceptible to frost. If frosts are likely to occur at a time close to when flower buds open, fruit development may be stopped even if the rest of the plant is unaffected.
- Some young seedlings are killed by frost.
- Tender, lush new growth is more susceptible to frost.

You need to know when frosts are likely to occur on a particular site, and select crops for that site which do not have a high risk of frost damage.

Day Length

Day length along with temperature is the most important factor in causing flower buds to form and fruit to develop. For some plants, the appropriate sequence of day length must take place for you to achieve a good crop. For other plants a minimum or maximum day length must occur before flower buds will form (e.g. African violets require at least 16 hours of daylight—or artificial light—for flowering to occur).

Brightness

For some plants, the intensity of light is just as critical as the length of light period. Many

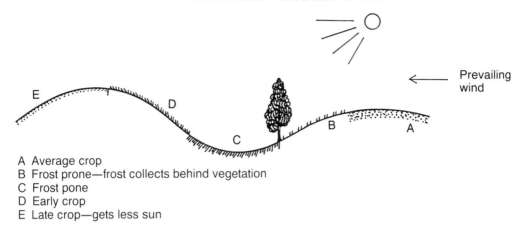

A Average crop
B Frost prone—frost collects behind vegetation
C Frost pone
D Early crop
E Late crop—gets less sun

Slope direction and local variations in landform will influence the timing of crops. Plants which are exposed to winds, frost and shade will have delayed flowering and fruiting.

vegetables and herbs do not produce the same quality or quantity of yield if light intensities are too low. Other plants must have lower light intensities, preferring shaded conditions.

A slope which catches the midday sun (i.e. north facing in the southern hemisphere) will have higher light intensities than one facing away from the afternoon sun. A site covered by tall trees or beside tall buildings will have lower light intensities than one in the open. A site in a valley may have lower light intensities than one on a ridge or a flat plain.

Rainfall

In low to medium rainfall areas, there is generally less need for hydroponic installations to be covered than in high rainfall areas, where the rainfall can dilute nutrient solutions or leach nutrients out of the system.

Humidity

Humid environments are suitable for some crops and unsuited to others. High humidity generally increases the likelihood of fungal diseases. Pollen may become more sticky and move around less easily in very humid situations. This can lead to a decrease in pollination of flowers which in turn may decrease the number of fruit forming.

Evaporation

Consider how fast water is lost through evaporation. This may influence your choice of hydroponic system. Some systems minimise loss through evaporation more than others.

Aspect

The best site will be relatively flat but with a slight slope to allow water to drain away. The site should not be prone to flooding.

A north-facing slope (in the southern hemisphere) will catch winter sun and be less prone to cold southerly winds or frosts. Sites in valleys are more prone to frosts, and will not become as warm in summer.

Wind

Wind can damage plants and greenhouses. In wind prone areas, it may be advisable to plant a windbreak to provide protection.

Some wind is needed for proper cross-pollination with certain crops. Air movement can also be beneficial by stopping disease spores from settling in one place and infecting a plant.

The crops, therefore, that you choose to grow should match the climatic patterns of the site.

Water Requirements

Water quality and quantity have a very important effect upon the viability of any hydroponic installation.

You may get water from town water supplies, a river or other watercourse, rainfall, dams, bores or even distilled sea water. In today's increasingly polluted world, no water supply can be guaranteed

A site with a good water supply is a distinct asset.

Variations in cropping due to slope direction. North-facing slopes will generally crop earlier than south-facing slopes which receive less winter sun.

to remain suitable for any great length of time. Watercourses in Australia are increasingly being affected by rising levels of salts. Acid rain is contaminating water supplies in Europe and America. You may need to face the prospect of treating water to remove impurities at some stage in the future if the quality of your supply is not very 'clean'.

Water with salt levels below 2500 ppm can be used for hydroponics, though much lower salt levels are preferred.

Some water supplies also contain very small quantities of other chemicals which will severely affect the crop potential. It is important that you know the quality of your water very well, and that you test it on a regular basis. Water quality can vary considerably over time, so even if your water tests out as being suitable when you first start, it may subsequently change, sometimes very quickly.

Quantity

Water requirements will vary greatly according to:

Size of plants—bigger plants generally need more water

Wind conditions—windy sites need more water

Humidity—high humidity reduces water requirements

Rainfall—if the system is in the open, natural rainfall may add to the water supply (though it may affect nutrient solution concentration)

Temperature—hot places lose more water through evaporation

Type of hydroponic system—recirculating systems need less water than run-to-waste systems
—highly absorbent media need less water than poorly absorbent ones
—there is less water loss when the root zone is surrounded by a water impermeable layer (e.g. NFT inside a fully enclosed pipe).

Most systems will use between 0.25 and 1.25 litres of water per day per square metre of growing surface, with the average unit normally using 0.5 to 0.6 litres per square metre per day.

Quality

Hard water is that which contains magnesium and calcium salts. In the presence of soaps, hard water forms a sludge. Hard water can be used for hydroponics provided it does not contain too much calcium carbonate.

Copper, zinc and several heavy metals such as lead or mercury can be found as contaminants in some waters. These can damage or kill plants. Excessive levels of these metals can be removed by slow filtration through a bed of calcareous material.

Free chlorine in large quantities (as found in some town water supplies) will damage or even kill plants. High levels can be removed by filtering through organic material such as straw.

Distilled salt water is suitable for hydroponics if obtained from solar distillation units. (NB: Sea water is distilled in metal stills in some parts of the world. In this situation, metals can contaminate the water at levels which are harmful to plants, though safe for human consumption.)

Very alkaline water can be treated by adding sulphuric acid to correct pH. (This is done before adding nutrients to make up the nutrient solution.)

Proximity to Markets

A large part of the cost of operating a hydroponic farm is the cost of transporting produce to market. You should consider the following:

- How close are you to the place where you will sell your produce?
- If using road transport, what is the quality of the roads?
  Does the route ever suffer traffic jams?
  Does the route ever flood?
- If using rail, how frequent is the rail service? Is the rail system viable for its operators and if not, is there a chance that services might be reduced?
- If using air or sea transport, how reliable and regular are the services?
- Does the produce need refrigeration or any other special treatment during transport and are those services available?
- If relying on contract services, are they dependable? Do they ever go on strike or break down?
- Will produce deteriorate during transport?
- Do you need to produce a truck or other transportation equipment (e.g. forklift etc.)?
- What will transportation cost?

Transportation to market may vary considerably depending on the site.

3 Alternatives

There are a bewildering number of choices to be made when deciding what type of system to use. This chapter is designed to help you choose the system that is right for you.

Water, Aggregate or Rockwool Culture

The first choice is whether to use water culture, aggregate culture or rockwool. All three are viable and used successfully with a large variety of crops in many different parts of the world.

Your choice should take into consideration the following:

- What is the cost of each and how readily available are materials in your area?

- Is rockwool made/sold locally? If not, what freight charges are involved in having it delivered?

- Is there a local source of sand or gravel which can be used, or do you need to pay high cartage costs?

- What types of plants will you grow?

Some plants require better aeration than others. Some systems provide better aeration than others, for example NFT systems.

Comparison of Cultural Systems

Rockwool	NFT	Aggregate
Modules are isolated (i.e. run to waste)	Modules are connected (solution recycled)	Modules may or may not be connected
Ability to easily flush out salt build up	Salts may occasionally build up on the sides of gullies, channels etc.	Nutrients may sometimes bind to some aggregate media i.e. scoria, pumice
Slabs are usually thrown away after one crop (suitable land fill tip site is needed)	No part of the system is thrown away	Medium is normally reused for many crops
Water air ratio changes between irrigations	Water air ratio remains constant	Water air ratio changes
Excess watering is needed (15%) to ensure driest slab remains wet	Water flow may become impaired by vigorous root systems i.e. cucurbits	Pressure needs to be high enough to provide adequate flows at the end of trickle irrigation runs
Nutrient imbalances not likely	Continual monitoring of nutrient solution is needed to prevent nutrient imbalances	
Suits most crops	Suits most crops except cucurbits	Suits most crops
Popular for carnations in Australia	Popular for lettuce in Australia and the UK	

Hydroponic Media

There are three main groups of hydroponic media, based on their origins:

1. Media derived from rock or stone
2. Media derived from synthetics
3. Organic media

General Characteristics

Media is the term given to the solid material(s) used to replace soil in aggregate culture and rockwool culture.

Hydroponic media must fulfill the following criteria:

- They must be chemically inert.
- They must be chemically stable.
- They must be clean.
- They must drain sufficiently freely not to create waterlogging problems.
- They must have adequate water-holding capacity.
- They must have adequate air-holding capacity.

Also
- Buffer capacity should be good—this is the ability of the media to resist changes in pH.
- It is preferable that cation exchange capacity is at least moderate to good.

Cation exchange capacity

Cations are atoms which have lost electrons. As such they are particles which have a positive charge. Many important plant nutrients occur in the nutrient solution as cations (i.e. potassium, calcium and magnesium). These particles will attach themselves to media particles which have a negative charge, hence staying in the media and being available to the plant roots for a longer period of time.

Organic matter such as peatmoss, and fine particles such as clay have a lot more negative charges on their surface, hence a greater ability to hold cations (higher cation exchange capacity) than larger sand or gravel particles. Media with a very low cation exchange capacity will require more frequent application of nutrients than ones with a higher cation exchange capacity. When nutrient solution is applied to a medium with low cation exchange capacity but high water holding capacity, the medium might remain moist, but the nutrients do not remain in it after the irrigation as well as in a medium with a high cation exchange capacity.

1. Media Derived from Rock or Stone

a. Vermiculite

This is a mineral derived from mica mined in South Africa and the USA. The mined mineral is treated in a number of ways including heating at temperatures of nearly 2000 degrees F to obtain the product used in hydroponics. Technically, vermiculite is hydrated magnesium aluminium iron silicate.

Vermiculite is very light and spongy in appearance. It weighs about 3.2. kg (7 lb) per cubic ft. It retains air, water and nutrients very well making it ideal for hydroponics. The pH of vermiculite is sometimes slightly acid or slightly alkaline, although rarely enough to pose much of a problem with growth. Its pH buffering capacity is very good (i.e. it resists changes in pH) and it has a relatively high cation exchange capacity.

Vermiculite needs to be mixed with other media to get the best results. Even though it retains air well, it can retain too much water (around 12 litres per cubic ft) for many plants. If used on its own it can after a year or so turn puggy (i.e. the structure can collapse). However, mixed with gravel or sand (no more than 40 or 50% vermiculite) it retains its structure, and drainage is improved to make it a more ideal medium.

Vermiculite is also used in the building industry for insulation. You should only use horticultural vermiculite in hydroponics. This is available in different grades:

No 1.—5 to 8 mm in diameter
No 2.—3 to 4 mm in diameter (this is the standard grade)
No 3.—1 to 2 mm in diameter
No 4.—0.75 to 1 mm in diameter (used only in seed germination)

b. Perlite

Perlite is like vermiculite, a processed mineral. It has excellent water holding properties but is less spongy and better drained than vermiculite. Perlite is made from a silicaceous volcanic rock treated at temperatures of 1400 degrees F to form sponge-like balls. Perlite is often used by itself or in a 50/50 mixture with vermiculite. (This type of mix can become too wet in some situations though.) Perlite can be neutral or slightly acid. It has poor pH buffering capacity and no cation exchange capacity.

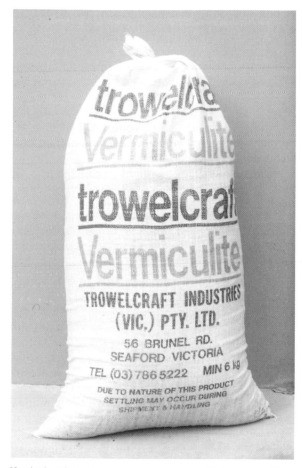

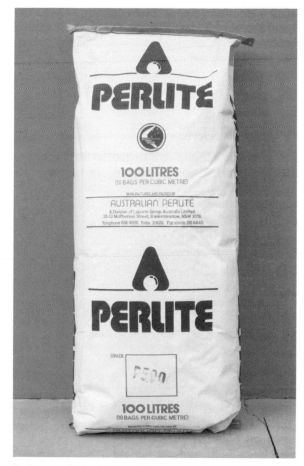

Horticultural grade vermiculite, normally sold in large bags. Most commonly used as an additive with other aggregates.

Perlite—available in large bags or prepacked polythene in hydroponic growbags.

As it is predominately white, algal growth may easily occur in perlite, and while this does not harm the plants it can clog up pipes etc. in a recirculating system. Perlite is excellent for plant propagation purposes. It can be expensive. Like vermiculite it is relatively light weight (2.5 to 3.5 kg (5.5-7.7 lb) per cubic ft).

c. Sand

Granitic or silica type sands should be used. Calcareous sands are very alkaline and unsuited to plant growth. Beach sand is not suitable because of high levels of salt in it. Some sands have a lot of dust or other fine material in them when purchased and these need to be washed out before it is used.

The best sand is the coarse granitic sand used by nurserymen for plant propagation and in fish aquariums. By itself sand will need frequent, if not constant flow of irrigation to prevent the plants drying out. It is often mixed with other water retaining materials though to obtain a balanced medium.

d. Gravel

Gravel is much the same as sand, only varying in particle size. Gravel particles are generally 2 to 15 mm in diameter, whereas sand particles are smaller, but still gritty to feel. Sand will hold water better than gravel.

e. Scoria

Scoria is a porous volcanic rock which can be obtained in a wide variety of grades (i.e. sizes or diameters). The physical properties of scoria are excellent, but its pH can very greatly according to

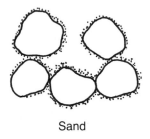

Sand

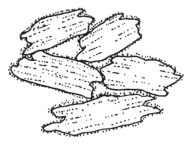

Vermiculite

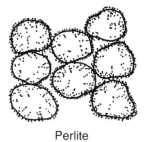

Perlite

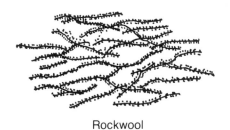

Rockwool

Indicates
water
penetration

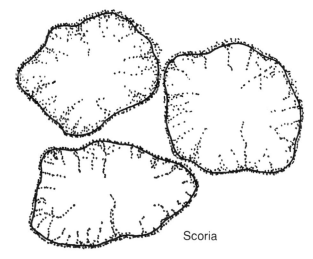

Scoria

Water penetration in different media.

Containers must have adequate drainage. This pot is particularly
good because of the larger than normal number of drainage
holes.

Vegetables in scoria. Scoria is a porous volcanic gravel. Initially it has an undesirably high pH, but this will drop and settle at an acceptable level if it is weathered for 6-12 months before use in a medium rainfall, cool temperature climate (e.g. Melbourne).

where it comes from (pH 7 to 10). The cost of scoria is usually dependent on the distance it has to be transported. If you are close to a scoria quarry it can be cheap; if you are some distance away it can be expensive. In Australia, scoria is available in parts of Victoria and north Queensland.

f. Pumice

This is a silicaceous volcanic rock, which is crushed and screened before use. Its properties are very similar to perlite except that it is heavier and does not absorb water as easily. Pumice is sometimes mixed with peat and sand to make a hydroponic medium.

g. Rockwool

Rockwool is made from heating rock into a molten state and spinning it into fine fibres to create a spongy, fibrous material which is used both for insulation (in the building industry) and in horticulture. Horticultural rockwool is processed differently from insulation rockwool. You should not use the insulation material in horticulture.

Horticultural rockwool is available in a loose fibre form (not unlike cotton wool or fleece), or in preformed slabs of varying shapes and depths. Rockwool slabs are more than 90% air space and so have the ability to hold large amounts of water while still retaining an extremely good level of aeration. This characteristic makes rockwool one of the most popular and commonly used media in commercial hydroponics in Australia, the Netherlands and several other countries.

Rockwool has no cation exchange capacity and very little effect on pH (i.e. the pH of the nutrient solution determines the pH of the root zone; the rockwool has virtually no effect).

h. Expanded Clay

Also called Leca (i.e. light expanded clay aggregate), this material is made by blending and bloating clay in rotary kilns. The material looks a little like hard terracotta balls. It has a low air-filled porosity and high water holding capacity. This material is now made in Australia.

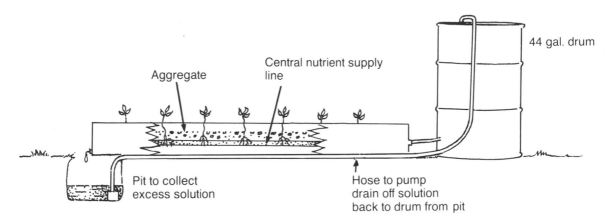

Simple automated aggregate bed system using a 44 gal. drum for nutrient feed.

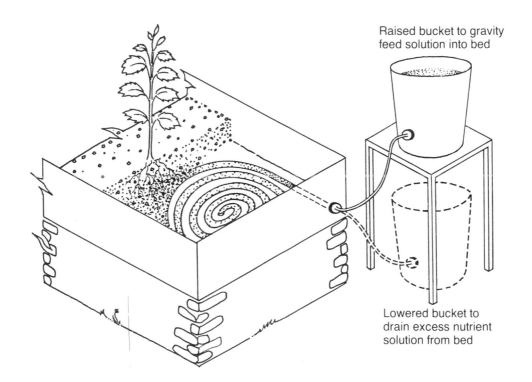

Simple manual system applying nutrient solution by gravity feed.

2. Media Derived from Synthetic Materials

a. Sponge Foams

Sponge-like materials are used increasingly for propagation (cuttings) in some parts of the world (e.g. Florida). These same materials have been successfully used in hydroponic culture. Foams are used commercially in hydroponics in the Netherlands and Canada. They are generally expensive.

b. Expanded Plastics

These materials are inert, and in many cases relatively inexpensive. Their major disadvantages are:

- They do not retain moisture or nutrient very well.
- They are very light weight and when mixed with other materials, often separate out (or float) to the top. (After a couple of months use, what was originally a mix will end up as a layer of the expanded plastic on top of the rest of the media.)
- They provide virtually no support for the plant (trellis is vital).

When used by themselves in a constant flow irrigation (automatic watering) situation, these materials can sometimes be quite successful.

Examples include polystyrene (bean bag) balls, hygropor (a mix of ureaformaldehyde and polystyrol), polystyrol etc. Ureaformaldehyde releases nitrogen slowly into solution through slow decomposition. If it is used for long periods, plants can be harmed by formaldehyde residues.

Good quality woodchips are an ideal medium for sawdust-based hydroponic systems. The individual particles are similar in size, providing a medium which is highly uniform in its physical characteristics.

3. Organic Media

a. Sawdust

Sawdust has been used extensively in commercial hydroponics in British Columbia and Canada, mainly because of its availability.

Hardwood sawdusts (e.g. from eucalypts) should be composted before use. Some softwood sawdusts should never be used because of highly toxic chemicals they contain. *Pinus radiata* sawdust has been successful for short term growing without composting (e.g. for propagation but not for growing a 6 month crop).

Sawdust will undergo decomposition while the crop is growing if not composted first, and throughout that process the bacteria will draw on nitrogen from the nutrient solution leaving insufficient for the plants.

Coarse sawdusts have been used successfully in potting soils in Australia, and should work in hydroponics. Fine sawdusts are preferred by the hydroponic growers in Canada, though fine sawdusts have caused problems when used in potting mixes in Australia.

Cation exchange capacity is good, but not as high as in peats.

Peat. Only coarse grade, high quality peat should be used in hydroponic systems.

b. Peat Moss

Peat moss is dug from swampy ground in cool temperate climates. It is the partially decomposed remains of plants (mainly mosses and sedges). The specific characteristics of peat can vary from one deposit to another though the following generalisations can be made:

- Peat has a high water holding capacity.
- Sphagnum peats generally have better aeration when wet than sedge peats.
- They are not totally free of nutrients. Some peats have a lot more mineral salts in them than others.

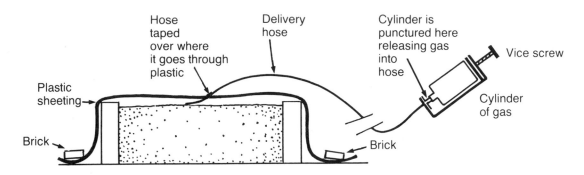

Chemical sterilisation using gas which is pumped into a sealed area.

- Black peat, which is more highly decomposed, is not suitable for hydroponics at all.
- Peat is always acidic (sometimes as low as 4.0).
- All peats have a high pH buffer capacity.
- They have a high cation exchange capacity.
- Peat repels water when it dries out. Be careful never to allow the surface of the medium to become completely dry.

Peat is useful as an additive to hydroponic media to raise the cation exchange capacity, particularly in run to waste systems, though it will bring micronutrients to the system which could upset the balance of the nutrient solution.

Only coarse grade, high quality peat should be used in hydroponic culture.

Sterilisation

Sterilisation with either chemicals or steam may be carried out to kill all pests and diseases in a hydroponic system or greenhouse prior to planting. This would commonly be done in the following situations:

- If a new system is installed in a locality where there may be diseases or pests.
- In a newly constructed greenhouse before planting the first crop.
- Where crops have been grown in the same medium for a long period, and disease or pests have built up in the system.

Steam Sterilisation

This is expensive if you have to buy a steam generator, however many greenhouse installations are heated with steam. It is relatively easy to install a steam converter on an existing boiler and run steam pipes to a greenhouse with outlet pipes at required intervals. Aggregate beds are easily treated by simply running a pipe with outlets along its length down the centre of a bed and covering the bed with a heat resistant cover. Application of steam at 180 degrees F for half an hour will sterilise about 20 cm depth of sawdust or peat, or 10 cm of 75% sand 25% peat. A permanent pipe laid below the surface at the bottom of a bed will give a better penetration of steam.

A steam sterilised bed can be used the day after treatment.

Chemical Sterilisation

a. With gas

This involves pumping chemical gases such as methyl bromide or chloropicrin into a sealed area. The area is generally covered with large plastic sheets and the gas released via a pipe or tube under the sheet. Alternatively an entire greenhouse can be sterilised if it is totally sealed from the outside.

After a predetermined period (usually a matter of days), the covers are lifted or the building is opened. The area must then be aired for a period to allow chemical residues to disappear before use.

b. With liquid

Formaldehyde, sodium hypochlorite and some other liquid preparations can be used to wash through hydroponic systems and over surrounding areas to kill pests and diseases. These are easy to use and relatively inexpensive, though you must be sure to wash away any residual chemicals before introducing plants into such areas.

4   Plant Nutrition

John Mason and Iain Harrison

Nutrient Formulas

A nutrient solution must contain nitrogen, phosphorus, potassium, magnesium, calcium and sulphur if plants are to make reasonable growth. These nutrients are all needed in significant quantities by all plants. Oxygen, hydrogen and carbon are also essential, however these are obtained by the plant from air and water.

A large number of other nutrients are also needed, but in very small amounts. These minor nutrients may find their way into a nutrient solution through impurities in the water or dust particles in the air, and that may be good enough for success in an amateur hydroponic grower's garden. The commercial grower, however, is well advised to use a nutrient solution with minute amounts of these minor nutrients added.

Minor nutrients such as iron, copper, boron, manganese, zinc, cobalt and molybdenum are just as important as the major nutrients; they are just used in much smaller quantities.

Preparing Nutrient Solutions

Nutrient solutions for small hydroponic systems can often be adequately prepared by adding some additional components to a standard, general fertiliser (e.g. 5 parts gypsum and 1 part epsom salts added to 6 parts of any powdered soluble plant food such as Thrive, Aquasol or Phostrogen). Sometimes it might be necessary to add a minute amount of micronutrient. Commercial hydroponic growers need a more accurate control of the components in a nutrient solution to achieve commercial success.

A large number of different nutrient formulas have been developed for use in hydroponics. Some give better results than others, however there is no single formula that outshines all the others. The success of each formula depends on the conditions in which it is used and on which plants are being grown.

To make a nutrient solution you need to know the relative amounts of the different nutrients a plant requires. The requirement is different for different types of plants. (This is discussed in Chapters 12–15.) You need to know what proportion of each chemical ingredient you are using is actually the nutrient (e.g. one chemical might contain 20% nitrogen and another chemical 45% nitrogen; you need less than half as much of the second chemical to supply the same amount of nitrogen).

You also need to know how soluble the chemicals you use are. Some chemicals need more water or more mixing than others.

Be aware of potential interactions between the chemicals you use. Some chemicals cannot be mixed with others—they react together and become something new: something you might not want in the solution, or something inert that can't be used by the plants you are growing.

Atomic weights of elements commonly used in hydroponic nutrient solutions

Element	Symbol	Atomic Wt	Element	Symbol	Atomic Wt
Boron	B	11	Manganese	Mn	55
Calcium	Ca	40	Molybdenum	Mo	96
Carbon	C	12	Nitrogen	N	14
Chlorine	Cl	35	Oxygen	O	16
Cobalt	Co	59	Phosphorus	P	31
Copper	Cu	64	Potassium	K	39
Hydrogen	H	1	Sodium	Na	23
Iron	Fe	56	Sulphur	S	32
Magnesium	Mg	24	Zinc	Zn	65

Calculating the Amount of Nutrient in a Chemical

The proportion by weight of a nutrient element in a nutrient salt can be calculated as follows:

- Write down the chemical formula of the salt. This should be on the product label. For example: ammonium sulphate $(NH_4)_2SO_4$

This simply means NH_4 plus NH_4 plus SO_4

In total then ammonium sulphate contains:
  2 nitrogen atoms
  8 hydrogen atoms
  1 sulphur atom
  4 oxygen atoms
- Look up the atomic weights of each of the elements in the nutrient salt and multiply them by the number of atoms of each element present in the chemical formula for that molecule.

For example: nitrogen (atomic weight = 14) 2 atoms × 14 = 28
  hydrogen (atomic weight = 1) 8 atoms × 1 = 8
  sulphur (atomic weight = 32) 1 atom × 32 = 32
  oxygen (atomic weight = 16) 4 atoms × 16 = 64
- Add up the total weights as calculated:
  For example 28 + 8 + 32 + 64 = 132
  The molecular weight of ammonium sulphate is therefore 132
- Take the total calculated weight of the nutrient element (i.e. in the above example this is 28 for nitrogen in ammonium sulphate) and divide this by the molecular weight of the nutrient salt (in this example that would be 132) giving 28/132 × 100/1 = 21.3%. This means that 21.3% of any quantity of ammonium sulphate is actually nitrogen.

Another example:
Sulphate of potash (potassium sulphate) is K_2SO_4
2 atoms of potassium . . . 2 × 39 = 78
1 atom of sulphur . . . 1 × 32 = 32
4 atoms of oxygen . . . 4 × 16 = 64
  Total = 174
Percentage of potassium = 78/174 × 100/1 = 44%

Note that many of the nutrient chemicals listed in the table in the next page contain sulphur. Sulphates are commonly used because plants tolerate large amounts of sulphur. An excess of unused sulphate around the plants' roots will be less damaging than an excess of chloride or something else.

All chemicals should be stored in a dry place until you are ready to use them. Choose your fertilisers not only on the basis of the nutrients they supply but also on how easy they are to obtain and how much they cost in terms of the amount of nutrient the fertilisers supply.

The most common way of describing the content of a nutrient solution is in parts per million (ppm). Since a gram of weight is equivalent to 1 cubic centimetre of water then 1 ppm is equivalent to 1 gram of water in 1 million cubic centimetres of water (1000 litres). 1000 litres is equivalent to about 264 US gallons. If you are using US measurements you can convert to ounces by dividing grams by 28.35 and litres to gallons by multiplying litres by 0.2642.

To make a solution containing, for example, 1 ppm of a particular nutrient you would need to add 1 gram of that nutrient to 1000 litres of water. To work out how much of the particular chemical you are using to supply that nutrient you would need to add to the 1000 litres of water, you need

Chemicals commonly used to prepare nutrient solutions

Chemical	Formula	Weight (g)	% of nutrients
Monoammonium phosphate	$NH_4H_2PO_4$	115.0	N(12%) P(27%)
Ammonium nitrate	NH_4NO_3	80.1	N(35%)
Ammonium sulphate (sulphate of ammonia)	$(NH_4)_2SO_4$	132.2	N(21%) S(24%)
Calcium sulphate (gypsum)	$CaSO_4.2H_2O_4$	172.2	Ca(22%) S(19%)
Magnesium sulphate (Epsom salts)	$MgSO_4.7H_2O$	246.5	Mg(9.9%) S(13%)
Phosphoric Acid	H_3PO_4	98.0	P(31.5%)
Monopotassium phosphate	KH_2PO_4	136.1	K(32.5%) P(26%)
Potassium chloride (muriate of potash)	KCl	74.6	K(52%)
Potassium sulphate (sulphate of potash)	K_2SO_4	174.3	K(44%) S(18%)
Superphosphate	$CaSO_4$ & $CaH_4(PO_4)_2$		Ca(20%) P(9%) S(12%)
Triple superphosphate	$CaH_4(PO_4)_2$		(Ca(13%) P(21%)
Iron sulphate	$FeSO_4.7H_2O$	278.0	Fe(20%) S(11.5%)

Amount of chemicals (in grams) used in making 1000 litres of nutrient solution

Chemical compound	Nutrient element supplied	Grams to give 1 ppm in 1000 L of water	Second element supplied
Ammonium sulphate	Nitrogen	4.7	
Calcium nitrate	Nitrogen	6.45	Calcium 1.36 ppm
	Calcium	4.7	Nitrogen 0.74 ppm
Potassium nitrate	Nitrogen	7.3	Potassium 2.6 ppm
	Potassium	2.8	Nitrogen 0.38 ppm
Sodium nitrate	Nitrogen	6.45	
Urea	Nitrogen	2.17	
Monopotassium phosphate	Potassium	3.53	Phosphorus 0.8 ppm
	Phosphorus	4.45	Potassium 1.26 ppm
Triple superphosphate	Phosphorus	4.78	Calcium 0.6 ppm
Calcium sulphate (gypsum)	Calcium	4.8	
Boric acid	Boron	5.64	
Copper sulphate	Copper	3.91	
Ferrous sulphate	Iron	4.96	
Manganese sulphate	Manganese	4.05	
Magnesium sulphate (Epsom salts)	Magnesium	10.25	
Molybdenum trioxide	Molybdenum	1.5	
Zinc sulphate	Zinc	4.42	

to know what percentage of the chemical is the actual nutrient. Based on the previous example this can be calculated as follows:

If the amount of nitrogen in ammonium sulphate is 23.1% then simply adding 1 gram of ammonium sulphate to the 1000 litres would only add 0.231 grams (23.1% of 1 gram) to the water. To get 1 gram of nitrogen you would need to work out the ratio between the amount of ammonium sulphate and the amount of nitrogen present in the ammonium sulphate. This can be simply done by dividing the molecular weight of ammonium sulphate by the weight of nitrogen found in the ammonium sulphate as follows:

$$132/28 = 4.7$$

This means that to obtain 1 gram of nitrogen you would need to add 4.7 grams of ammonium sulphate to the 1000 litres. This conversion factor of 4.7 remains constant for the supply of nitrogen using ammonium sulphate as a source, so that if you wanted for example a solution containing 200 ppm of nitrogen you would simply multiply 200×4.7 to give 940 grams of ammonium sulphate being required to go in 1000 litres of water. This technique can be used just as simply for the other chemicals used in hydroponics stock solutions. (See table on page 29.)

Preparing a Solution

A simple means of preparing your nutrient solution is as follows:

- First weigh nutrient chemicals individually.
- Lay the chemicals out in separate piles and check each noting the colour of the chemical and relative sizes of the amounts, to ensure the proportions make sense and no mistakes have been made.
- Be particularly careful that no chemical component is left out or weighed twice.
- Accuracy of weighing should be within plus or minus 5% (within this range the effect on plants will be neglible).
- After all of this has been done, add the chemicals to the mixing tanks and stir vigorously until dissolved (the order in which the chemicals are added is unimportant, but it is extremely important to dissolve less soluble salts such as superphosphate as much as possible. There will always be some material which doesn't dissolve,

but this is generally not enough to be significant.
- After mixing the nutrients the pH may need adjusting (see the section on pH).
- Micronutrients should always be added *after* pH is adjusted in the solution.

Example Solutions

The following solutions give an indication of the types of combinations of chemicals that are commonly used.

Example 1

All quantities are based on using pure water. Two concentrated stock solutions are made up as shown below:

Solution 1
To 100 litres of water add:

Calcium nitrate	7.5 kg

Solution 2
To 100 litres of water add:

Potassium nitrate	9.0 kg
Potassium dihydrogen phosphate	3.0 kg
Magnesium sulphate	6.0 kg
Iron chelate EDTA	300 g
Manganese sulphate	40 g
Borax	37 g
Copper sulphate	8 g
Zinc sulphate	4 g
Ammonium molybdate	1 g

Dilution

Each stock solution should be diluted to 1 in 100.
Do not mix the concentrated stock solutions.

When you are ready to apply the nutrient solution, mix the diluted stock solutions then.

This is because fertilisers containing calcium will react with any containing phosphate in a stock solution to form calcium phosphate. This will precipitate out of the solution and fall to the bottom of the tank or container holding the solution, where it forms a sludge. The majority of the calcium and phosphate in the stock solution becomes unavailable to your plants and the insoluble calcium phosphate sludge may block irrigation lines and nozzles. It is also important not to mix calcium nitrate in a stock solution with magnesium sulphate because calcium sulphate will precipitate out of the solution. The majority of other chemicals commonly used in stock solutions can be mixed together, however care should be taken when using previously untried formulations that precipitation doesn't occur.

Example 2
Bengal basic formula used in India.

Chemical	Grams per 1000 litres of water
Sodium nitrate	170
Ammonium sulphate	85
Calcium sulphate	43
Superphosphate*	100
Potassium sulphate	114
Trace elements#	0.5

* Single form
\# Trace element mixture consists of 5 g of zinc sulphate, 5 g of copper sulphate, 13 g of boric acid, 15 g of manganese sulphate and 19 g of iron sulphate.

Example 3
A widely used formula in the USA is one devised by Hoagland and Arnon at the University of California.

Chemical	Grams per 1000 litres of water
Calcium nitrate	1181
Potassium nitrate	505.5
Monopotassium phosphate	136.1
Magnesium sulphate	493

Alternative formulation

Calcium nitrate	1181
Potassium nitrate	505.5
Monoammonium phosphate	115.0
Magnesium sulphate	493.0

To both formulations are added a trace element solution comprising the following:

Chemical	Grams to make 1 litre of stock solution
Boric acid	2.86
Manganese chloride	1.81
Zinc sulphate	0.22
Copper sulphate	0.08
Molybdic acid	0.02

This is sufficient stock to make 1000 litres of the dilute nutrient solution. An iron stock solution is also required. This should contain 1 gram of actual

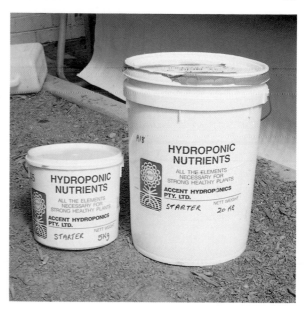

Hydroponic nutrient is commonly purchased in premixed powder form.

iron per litre of stock solution. One litre of iron stock is sufficient for 1000 litres of dilute nutrient solution.

The above stock solutions are just a few of the many solutions that have been developed for general use. Each plant, however, has different nutritional requirements, and these may vary at different stages of the plant's growth. For example when the plant is making a lot of leaf growth then nitrogen requirements are generally higher than when the plant is fruiting. Stock solutions can generally be modified to some degree to be suitable for the majority of cultivated plants, however some may require specific formulations. Chapters 12–15 list particular nutrient requirements for many of the commonly grown vegetable, berry, fruit, herb and flower crops that can be grown hydroponically.

Educated Guesses

When you are not sure about the type and quantity of nutrients to be used then some relatively simple techniques can give you a clue:

1. The most suitable ranges of nutrient concentrations for a nutrient solution appear in the table on the next page.

2. *Experimentation*—simply try growing a few plants of the crop you are interested in. If these

Nutrient element	Concentration (mg/litre or ppm)
Nitrogen (nitrate)	70–400
Nitrogen (ammonium)	0–31
Phosphorus	30–100
Potassium	100–400
Calcium	150–400
Magnesium	25–75
Iron	0.5–5
Boron	0.1–1
Zinc	0.02–0.2
Copper	0.1–0.5
Manganese	0.5–2
Molybdenum	0.01–0.1

show recognisable signs of nutrient deficiency or toxicity then you can adjust your nutrient solution accordingly. It is important to be careful of your solution pH as this will affect nutrient take up in the plant (see section on pH).

3. Growers who are capable of testing the nutrient status of their run-off solution can determine which nutrients are being taken up by the plants in what quantities, and adjust their nutrient solutions accordingly.

4. A rough indication of nutrient requirements can often be obtained by consideration of the type of crop you are growing. For example crops with a high percentage of leafy material are likely to have medium to high nitrogen requirements, while root crops often require moderate to high levels of phosphorus. Comparisons can often be drawn with similar growing crops.

5. Many agricultural and horticultural journals and texts provide nutrient advice and research results on particular crop species. It is often possible to get a good indication of the nutrient requirements of particular plants from these. A good example is the text *Plant Analysis* edited by D. J. Reuter and J. B. Robinson (Inkata Press, Melbourne), which gives a strong indication of nutrient requirements for a wide range of crop plants, based on analysis of the relationship between yields and nutrient concentrations in plant tissues.

Propagation

If nutrition is needed during propagation, then a weaker solution should be used, i.e. the above solutions should be diluted by a further 1 in 4.

What is pH?

pH is a measurement of the hydrogen ion concentration in a particular medium, such as water, soil, gravel etc. More simply it refers to the acidity or alkalinity of that medium. The pH is measured on a logarithmic scale ranging from 0 to 14 with 7 being considered neutral, above 7 being considered alkaline and below 7 as acid.

The pH of a medium or a nutrient solution is important to plant growth. Each particular plant has a preferred pH range in which it grows. If a plant is subjected to a pH outside of its preferred range at the least its growth will be retarded, or it may even die. Very low pH (less than pH = 4.5) and very high pH ·conditions (above pH = 9) can directly damage plant roots.

Very high and low pH values can also affect plants as follows:

1. As the pH of a medium changes so does the availability of nutrients. The majority of nutrients are most available at a pH range of 6 to 7.5. Somewhere in this range is generally considered to be the ideal for growing the majority of plants, although there are plants that prefer higher or lower pH conditions. In some circumstances, particularly at very low or high pH conditions, some nutrients may become 'locked' in the medium, becoming unavailable for plant growth. The nutrients may be there in the medium but the plant can't use them. At very low pH condition toxic levels of some nutrients such as manganese and aluminium may be released.

2. As the pH of some media is raised more negative charges are produced on some colloid surfaces, making them capable of holding more cations. This allows some media to hold larger quantities of nutrients. The majority of hydroponic media are not affected in this way as they are basically inert materials such as sand and gravel, however media that contain clays or some of those derived from volcanic materials can be affected.

3. Like plants, microorganisms have a prefered pH range in which they thrive. Altering the pH may severely affect the populations of both beneficial and detrimental microorganisms. For example the bacteria that convert ammonium to nitrogen prefer a pH above 6. Most mycorrhizal fungi prefer a pH range between 4 and 8.

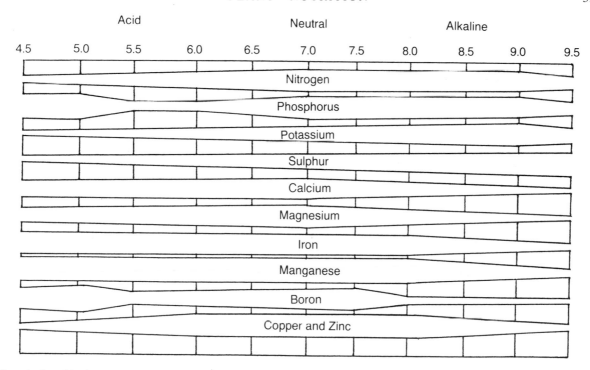

Truog's chart: Nutrient availability at different pH levels. (From Truog, E., *US Dep. Agr. Yearbook*, 1941-47, pp. 566-576)

Adjusting the pH

Before using a solution you should test its pH. Ready to use nutrient solution should normally have a pH between 6 and 6.5 (though for some types of plants the ideal pH is higher or lower than this).

If necessary the pH can be changed as follows:

- Adding lime (or some other calcareous component) will raise pH.
- Adding diluted sulphuric or nitric acid will lower pH.
- Ammonium salts will acidify (e.g. ammonium sulphate).
- As some nutrients are absorbed and others are left in the root environment, the pH will change.
- Careful addition of caustic soda will increase pH.

Some types of aggregate media will affect the pH of the nutrient solution and root zone, for example peat is acidic and freshly mined scoria is alkaline. If the medium is to be wet initially with nutrient solution then the pH of the solution used, for the initial wetting only, should be lowered or raised when the medium has a high or low pH.

Conductivity

Conductivity is a measure of the rate at which a small electric current flows through a solution.

When there is a greater concentration of nutrients, the current will flow faster, and when there is a lower concentration, the current flows more slowly.

By measuring conductivity, you can determine just how strong or weak a nutrient solution is. A conductivity meter is used to make such measurements.

Conductivity can be measured in any of the following units:

EC, short for 'electroconductivity'. EC is expressed as either millimhos per centimetre (i.e. mMho/cm), or as millisiemen per centimetre (i.e. mS/cm).
Note: 1mMho/cm = 1 mS/cm

CF, short for 'conductivity factor'. CF is expressed on a scale of 1 to 100, where 0 stands for pure water containing no nutrient and 100 represents maximum strength of nutrient salts in solution.

EC is generally measured at 25 degrees C, and most literature and recommendations are based upon the nutrient solution being at that temperature. If the temperature of a solution is raised, the EC will increase, even though there are no extra nutrients added. If the temperature drops, the EC will decrease. It is possible to calculate the change in EC when temperature changes by multiplying the EC by a conversion factor (refer to table below).

Temperature conversion factors for determining EC at temperatures varying from the standard of 25 degrees celsius

°C	Conversion factor
15	1.247
20	1.112
22	1.064
25	1.0
27	0.96
30	0.907

Conductivity and Hydroponics

- Conductivity needs to be regularly monitored in a hydroponic system.
- Different plants have preferred conductivity levels at which they will grow their best. These levels can very during a crop's life.
- A grower should predetermine the desired conductivity for the crop being grown, and any changes in that desired level from one stage of a crop to the next.
- As a solution uses nutrient, the EC will drop. When a drop is detected, nutrient should be added to the solution to bring it back to the desired level.

Detecting Deficiencies and Toxicities

An important means of managing the nutrient requirements of your plants is the ability to recognise signs of nutrient deficiencies or toxicities, ideally as early as possible so that such problems can be rectified with minimal impact on crop yields. Such recognition can be aided by the use of simple keys such as the following one.

Key to Symptoms of Nutrition Deficiency

Symptoms   *Deficiency*
A. Lower leaves mainly affected. The affect may occur on one part or over the whole plant.

B. Effects appear over whole plant; lower leaves go dry; foliage turns light or dark green.
C. Plant light green, lower leaves yellow, drying to light brown colour, stalks short and slender if element is deficient in later growth stages.
Nitrogen
CC. Plant dark green, often develops red and purple colour, lower leaves sometimes yellow, drying to greenish brown or black.   **Phosphorus**
BB. Effects mostly localised; mottling or chlorosis, with or without spots of dead tissue on lower leaves, little or no drying up of lower leaves.
C. Mottled or chlorotic leaves, typically may redden, sometimes with dead spots, tips and margins turned and cupped upwards, stalks slender.
Magnesium
CC. Mottled or chlorotic leaves with large or small spots of dead tissue.
D. Spots of dead tissue small, usually on tips and between veins, more marked at margins of leaves.
Potassium
DD. Spots spread over the whole plant, rapidly enlarging; they commonly affect areas between veins and eventually spread to affect the veins also; leaves thick, stalks develop shortened internodes.
Zinc
AA. Newer or bud leaves affected, symptoms localised.
B. Terminal bud dies, following appearance of distortion at tips or base of young leaves.
C. Young leaves of terminal bud at first hooked finally dying back at tips and margins, stalk finally dies at terminal bud.   **Calcium**
CC. Young leaves of terminal bud become light green at bases and finally break down here, later growth leaves become twisted, stalk finally dies back at terminal bud.   **Boron**
BB. Terminal bud commonly remains alive.
D. Young leaves permanently wilted without spotting or marked chlorosis, stalk just below tip will bend over in acute deficiency.   **Copper**
DD. Young leaves not wilted.
E. Dead spots uncommon, young leaves chlorotic (yellow), main veins green, yellowing can spread to older leaves.   **Iron**
EE. Young leaves and veins yellow.   **Sulphur**
EEE. Dead spots scattered over leaf, smallest veins green giving chequered effect.   **Manganese**

Salinity Build-up

When a plant uses a nutrient from a chemical 'salt' molecule supplied in a nutrient solution, it is in fact only using one part of that molecule. The remaining part of the molecule generally stays in the hydroponic system. It may be used by the plant, but more commonly it builds up in the system, and eventually can reach a level of concentration where it causes damage to the plant.

This is referred to as 'salt build-up' or a 'salinity' problem. Salinity problems are most common when media with a high cation exchange capacity are used, or in a closed system using the same nutrient solution for an extended period.

Salinity problems will sometimes be visible. If you see a white caking around pipes, water outlets, or on the surface of the media, this indicates the problem is reaching the danger level.

Salinity can be cured or prevented by simply leaching the salt build-up out of the system by washing it through with water. This water must of course be drained out of the system to remove the unwanted salts.

Soil Life and Hydroponics

In soil there are many different types of relationships which develop between plant roots and microorganisms such as bacteria and fungi. Some such relationships can be of great benefit to the plant, helping it to secure nutrients from the soil. When a plant is grown in hydroponics, free of all harmful microorganisms, it is free of the beneficial organisms also.

Some plants must have certain microorganisms, such as mycorrhizal fungi, living around their roots in order for them to grow properly. Orchids and mushrooms are two examples. Such plants will not perform in hydroponics if the root environment is very clean!

A number of microorganisms have the ability to convert atmospheric nitrogen into forms such as ammonium or nitrate which can then be utilised by plants. These microorganisms include Rhizobium bacteria, some actinomycetes and some blue-green algae. Rhizobium bacteria have a symbiotic relationship with leguminous-type plants in which they provide a source of nitrogen to the plant and receive in return other nutrients such as carbohydrates. The nitrogen is 'fixed' by the Rhizobium bacteria in nodules on the roots of the legumes and is thus directly available to the plants. Innoculation of media deficient in Rhizobium bacteria can be achieved by grinding the root nodules from mature legumes and mixing them in a small amount of water and then adding the mix to the nutrient solution.

It has been suggested by Cooper (*The ABC of NFT*, 1979, Grower Books, London) that only very low concentrations of nitrogen are required in the nutrient solution if the supply is maintained, and that it may be possible to provide an optimal balance of nitrogen-fixing plants to non-fixing plants in a cropping system, whereby nitrogen exuded from the roots of the nitrogen-fixing plants would be carried by the recirculating solution to the other plants.

Organic Hydroponics

Organic fertlisers such as manures are complex chemicals which require microorganisms to act upon them and break them down into simpler forms before the plant can take them in. Such fertilisers cannot be used in hydroponics unless the appropriate microorganisms are first introduced to the hydroponic root environment.

Hydroponics is possible with organic chemicals if the root zone is inoculated with appropriate decomposing microorganisms, however the commercial potential of organic hydroponics seems very uncertain for the near future.

5   NFT Culture

Nutrient Film Technique (NFT) is a method of soilless culture where plants are grown bare rooted in long narrow channels which enclose a shallow stream of nutrient solution. The nutrient solution flows continuously through the channel (being recycled from the bottom to the top end by a pump). The plant roots grow into a dense mat in the channel and the foliage sits on top, sometimes provided with support by a trellis system.

The channels are made of water-tight material such as PVC or plastic film. They are laid on a slight slope to allow the nutrient solution to flow from top to bottom (supported by a rack or on a bench). The channel is enclosed as much as possible, with openings only needed for the top growth of the plants to come through.

Even though the majority of space inside the channel is air space, because it is enclosed a very high level of humidity is created in which roots can still grow (in fact this ensures adequate levels of oxygen in the root zone, which can sometimes be a problem when plants are grown in soil).

A typical NFT system thus is made up of the following components:

1. Gullies along which nutrient solution flows continuously and in which plant roots grow.

2. A catchment pipe into which the gullies discharge solution.

3. A catchment tank, in which solution collects at the bottom of the gully system.

4. A pump to draw the water from the catchment tank and return it to the top of the gully system.

5. A delivery pipe to return solution from the catchment tank to the top of the gully system.

6. Tanks containing concentrated nutrient solutions or acidic solution (which can be injected into the dilute nutrient solution as required to adjust the pH or nutrient levels).

7. Sensing devices to measure pH and EC in the nutrient solution, connected to control devices (such as solenoid valves) which release additives into the nutrient solution when required, in order to maintain a properly balanced solution.

8. Benching (or some other construction) to support the gullies and maintain the required slope.

Disadvantages

- If the flow of nutrient solution stops, the roots will dry out and become stressed very quickly.
- In a newly planted system where the channels are exposed to strong sunlight, they can heat up faster than the root zone would heat in aggregate or rockwool. (N.B. The continuous flow of solution does have a cooling effect however.)
- NFT channels can become blocked by roots of vigorous-growing plants.

NFT System Choices

Header Tank or Direct Pumping

The nutrient solution is normally stored in a sump or catchment tank which collects the run-off from NFT channels. The nutrient solution can be delivered from the sump to the top of each channel in one of two ways:

Directly—where it is pumped into feeder tubes

which supply the top of each channel

Via a header tank—where it is pumped into a secondary tank placed at a level higher than the channels. The nutrient solution then flows via a system of delivery tubes into the channels by gravity.

The advantage of a header tank is that it will continue to operate for some time after the pump ceases to operate (if there is some problem with the pump).

Gully Construction Materials

Some materials can have a phytotoxic effect in that chemicals in the material dissolve into the flowing solution and deter plant growth. Gullies or channels have been successfully constructed from all of the following:

1. PVC house guttering
2. Square PVC plumbers' downpipe with holes cut in the top for plants.
3. Circular PVC drainage pipe with holes cut in the top for plants.
4. Corrugated fibreglass sheeting with an overlay of flat plastic.
5. Asphalt-coated wood.
6. Folded polythene film pinned at the top to make a tube.
7. Concrete formed into gullies on the surface of the ground.

Polythene Gullies

• Polythene is totally inert and causes no phytotoxic effect on plant roots.
• A heavier gauge polythene allows gullies to be reused. Lighter gauge polythene is cheaper, but must be discarded after one crop.
• In England 600-1000 gauge polythene is used, black on one side and white on the other side. A 65 to 80 cm wide sheet is used. The sheet is laid out on the permanent surface (where levels have previously been established), with the white surface underneath. The sides are then folded up and stapled together. The top of each end is then stapled. The nutrient solution is delivered by a micro-irrigation tube at the top end and unused solution collects into a return pipe at the bottom.
• Black polythene (both sides) has been used, though this will heat up the solution if exposed to direct sunlight and can 'cook' the roots in a young crop over summer. Once the crop grows and begins to shade the plastic this problem

disappears. In hot conditions, shading may be used in the interim period until the crop is large enough.
• Pre-creased gusset channel made from polythene sheet is available in some countries (e.g. the UK). This is PVC already folded into a channel shape which can be rolled out on a prepared surface and periodically joined together along the top rim through existing holes using a supplied clip.

PVC gullies

• Rigid PVC has no phytotoxic effect on plant roots.
• Flexible PVC has at times had a phytotoxic effect on plant roots.
• Rigid white PVC plumbers' pipe has often been used with holes cut out to insert plants.
• Specially designed products made from rigid PVC are available in Australia and some other countries (e.g. Vinidex Hydro Channel consisting of rectangular growing channels with a variety of different lids and end caps. This is available in two different sizes, in 6 metre lengths, from Vinidex, PO Box 299, Gordon, NSW, Australia 2072).

Concrete

Permanent channels can be formed in concrete, and covers laid over the surface with holes cut to insert plants in.

Concrete gully systems have been operated successfully on a commercial basis in both England and the West Indies.

Corrugated PVC or Fibre Glass

Corrugated sheet, as used in roofing, is sometimes used as a base for NFT gullies. Solution can be fed in the top and flow down to the low points of the corrugations. A second layer needs to be established above to support the plants.

Metal Gullies

Metal piping should not be used because it will corrode. The corrosion leads to impurities in the system which can upset pH and nutrient balances, clog small pipes (when flakes of metal chip off) and in some cases cause toxicity to plants.

Modified NFT

A modified form of NFT often used, involves filling the NFT channel with a very coarse aggregate such as gravel. There is still a continuous flow of nutrient

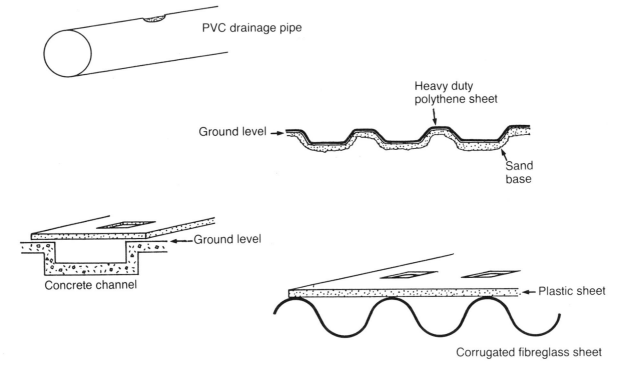

PVC drainage pipe

Heavy duty polythene sheet

Ground level →

Sand base

Ground level

Concrete channel

Plastic sheet

Corrugated fibreglass sheet

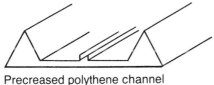

Precreased polythene channel

Semi rigid plastic

Reflective aluminium foil

Air pocket

Metal →

Universal NFT Channel

Alternative ways of constructing NFT channels.

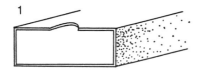

1

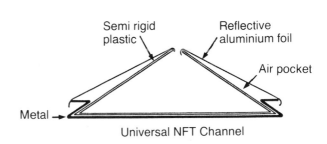

2

Gravel

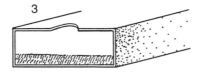

3

Capillary mat

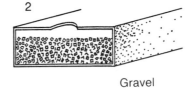

Three ways of treating NFT channel:
1. Enclosed channel with no insert
2. Modified channel filled with gravel
3. Channel with capillary mat.

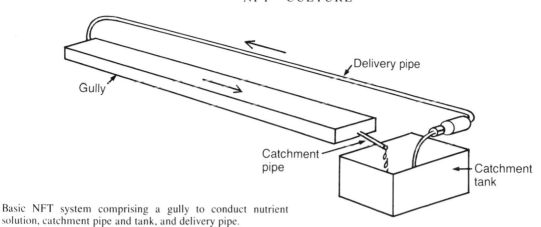

Basic NFT system comprising a gully to conduct nutrient solution, catchment pipe and tank, and delivery pipe.

solution through the gully, and with a very coarse aggregate that flow is not impaired. Major advantages are:

- Moisture adheres to the aggregate. This increases the availability of moisture in the higher layers of the channel and should the flow of nutrient stop, the roots will be kept moist for a period until the flow can be restarted.
- Temperature fluctuations are reduced. The aggregate stops the channel heating up or cooling down so fast.
- The aggregate supplies support to the plants.

Solution Delivery

Normally solution is delivered as a continuous flow; but sometimes it is only delivered for a few minutes, then stopped for 15 to 60 minutes before flowing again. In the case of plants which require very good aeration, this intermittent supply may be used to increase aeration in the root zone (particularly critical in established plants where the root system can clog the channel and slow down water supply).

Capillary Matting

No matter how carefully constructed the base of an NFT channel is, you will still almost always get some fall from one side of the channel to the other. Capillary matting is sometimes placed on the bottom of the channel to even out the flow of solution. The solution is soaked up by the mat and spread right across the channel, preventing the solution from flowing on one side of the channel leaving the other side dry.

The capillary mat material must be absorbent, physically stable and chemically inert. There have

been cases of phytotoxicity reported through use of inappropriate materials for capillary matting. Materials used successfully include: cellulose fibre, rockwool and various man made fibres.

Channel Width and Length

The width for a single row of plants should normally be between 10 and 15 cm. For a double row of plants the channel should be 25 to 30 cm wide. Multi-channels, more than two rows wide, are also used at times (where there is no great problem with plants growing in close proximity to each other).

Channels should never be more than 30 m long (20 m is preferred). This is because plants in the upper parts of long channels will remove a lot of nutrients from the solution before it reaches plants in the lower sections. Also in long channels strong root systems may impede the flow rates in lower sections and create differences in water levels between the beginning and end of the channel.

Slope

The depth of the nutrient solution in the channel should not normally be more than a few millimetres. The major part of the root mat should not be submerged in solution.

Normally 1:150 or greater slope is required to achieve a proper flow of solution where capillary mat is used on a flat bottom. If the bottom of the channel is made using corrugated sheeting a stiff capillary mat can be laid over the top allowing a free flow of solution along the channel below. If the bottom is flat though, the flow along the bottom will be slowed by the capillary mat, hence requiring a greater slope along the channel to

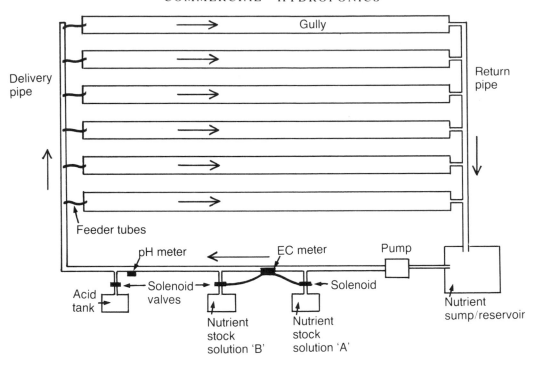

Automatic NFT system layout.
Note: EC meter connected into irrigation line will sense when the conductivity drops and automatically open solenoid valves, releasing nutrient solution from the stock tanks.
pH meter similarly senses change in pH and releases acid into the irrigation line when needed.
Arrows indicate the direction of nutrient solution flow.

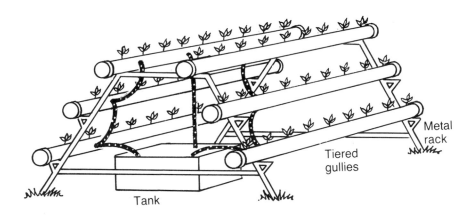

NFT in PVC pipes tiered on a metal rack. Solution is pumped from the reservoir via a submersible pump, to the high end of each channel. It is then collected at the low end and returned via pipes to the reservoir.

PVC channels growing commercial lettuce crop.

achieve the same flow rate.

Where capillary mat is not used, the slope can be as little as 1:200 to 1:250.

The rate at which solution is fed into the channels should be as great as is possible without increasing the depth of nutrient solution to more than a few millimetres in the channel. This can only be determined by trial and error for each situation.

Temperature

Ideally a solution should be kept at between 18 and 22 degrees C for most plants. There is a danger of solution overheating inside channels if they receive too much direct sun in the early stages of a crop. As the crop develops though, it will shade the channel and this problem becomes less likely.

Nutrition

It has for many years been considered that all plants require around 20 nutrient elements for their growth, and some plants might require a few more. Less than ten elements are known to be used in large quantities, and these are what make up the bulk of any nutrient being fed to plants growing in NFT. The remaining nutrients are generally supplied in either tiny quantities, or not supplied at all. It is assumed that dust in the air or impurities in the system will supply these tiny quantities of minor nutrients. This is however not always the case, and minor nutrient deficiencies can have drastic effects on the crop produced (even though they are only needed in small amounts).

Recent research has actually found that up to 93 elements are in fact needed to maximise the flavour in fruit and vegetables. (Potassium and magnesium are particularly important to the flavour of strawberries, though many other nutrient elements still have a contributing effect on the resulting quality.)

Stoughton in 1969 recommended that nutrient solutions for general use in NFT should have the major nutrients at the following levels:

Nitrogen: 100 to 300 mg/litre
Potassium: 120 to 250 mg/litre

Asher and Ozanne in 1967 tested 14 different plant species in NFT and found that eight of these species achieved maximum yields at 0.9 mg/litre concentration for potassium. The remaining species produced their best yields at concentrations of 3.7 mg/litre of potassium.

Trials on NFT (at GCRI in the UK) have shown most plant species commonly grown in NFT will in fact tolerate a wide range of nutrient concentrations. Trials have shown no significant loss in yield caused by varying nitrogen concentrations between a low of 10 mg/litre and a high of 320 mg/litre. Note though: not all nutrients will produce a similar response over such a wide range and not all plant species respond similarly.

Recommendations for nutrient concentration for tomatoes in NFT culture
(*Source*: Dept Agriculture, UK, 1981)

Nutrient (concentration in mg/litre)

	Minimum	*Optimum*	*Maximum*
N	50	150–200	300
P	20	50	200
K	50	300–500	800
Ca	125	150–300	400
Mg	25	50	100
Fe	3	6	12
Mn	0.5	1	2.5
Cu	0.05	0.1	1
Zn	0.05	0.1	2.5
B	0.1	0.3–0.5	1.5
Mo	0.1	0.05	0.1
Na	—	—	250
Cl	—	—	400

Solution depositing into the collection pipe at the ends of the NFT channels—from there it returns to the nutrient tank.

Mixing Nutrients

In many instances, the total nutrients are supplied as a single mix, either in powdered form or predissolved in solution. These are obviously the easiest to work with, however, in some instances the solution is delivered as two or three separate components, each one mixed into the system from separate holding tanks.

Some nutrients used in NFT will react together causing precipitation. For this reason, operations may need to use two or three different tanks, each containing separate and different stock solutions which, when mixed together in a predetermined ratio, will produce a balanced nutrient solution. E.g. Salts which are not very soluble, such as calcium phosphate or calcium sulphate, tend to precipitate out of solution very easily.

A typical situation might involve 3 tanks:

- one containing calcium nitrate
- a second containing most other nutrients
- a third containing diluted acids, which might be a source of nutrients such as nitrogen and potassium as well as being used to alter pH.

Research

Reported in *Grower* magazine 6 July 1989:

St Katelijne-Waver Research Station in Belgium conducted research to determine optimum conditions for growing tomatoes in NFT. Plants were started in rockwool propagating cubes and then, in mid-winter, some earlier than others, placed in NFT channels under a continuous flow of nutrient solution.

Those plants planted later yielded stronger crops earlier in the season, but weaker yields later on.

Those planted earlier took longer to give good yields, but continued producing crops later in the season.

Some were propagated in propagating foam (i.e. like sponge) and compared with rockwool. Those grown in foam did not crop as heavily as those propagated in rockwool.

Stopping the circulation of the solution for 15 minutes each hour caused a reduction in yield.

Reducing the pH from 6.0 to 5.0 had no significant effect on the time or quantity of yield.

6 Rockwool Culture

Rockwool is a fibrous material produced by melting rock and spinning it into threads. Developed in Denmark during the late 1960s for horticultural use, it was marketed under the trade name 'Grodan'. Its commercial use expanded throughout the late 1970s, especially in western Europe for the production of glasshouse vegetables and cut flowers. In Holland use of rockwool for vegetable production expanded from 100 ha in 1979 to 900 ha in 1982 and 2250 ha in 1987, with another nearly 600 ha of flower crops in 1987. In England around 85% of hydroponic growing is in rockwool compared to 11% in NFT. Major crops include tomatoes, cucumbers, eggplants and capsicums.

Today rockwool is marketed under several different names including the original 'Grodan'. In Australia, Bradford Insulation (part of CSR Limited) has marketed an Australian rockwool, known by the trade mark 'Growool', since mid 1982. About one third (around 30 ha) of Australian hydroponic growing area is comprised of rockwool slabs. Major Australian crops include carnations, tomatoes, cucumbers, gerberas, strawberries and roses.

How Rockwool is Made

Rockwool has been manufactured as an acoustic and heat insulation material for over 50 years. The production technology has been extensively improved over this period, but the basic product has remained virtually unchanged.

The raw materials are natural rocks such as basalt, plus coke as the fuel. These are fed into a blast furnace through which air is blown so that the coke burns and lifts the temperature to over 1600 degrees C. The rocks melt to form a type of lava which settles to the bottom of the furnace and is tapped off.

The stream of lava flows onto a series of high speed rotors. These spin off molten droplets which lengthen into fibres and are then cooled by a blast of air. Binder is sprayed into this air stream which also carries the fibres clear of the rotors and deposits them on a conveyor as a thick felt. The felt is conveyed along a production line where it is pressed, hardened, trimmed and finally cut into slabs. One manufacturing aspect of the rock-fibre mat is that the fibres orientate in a horizontal plane. This has implications that are important when the material is used for horticultural purposes.

Insulation rockwool and fibreglass are useless for horticultural purposes. However, the rockwool manufacturing process can be modified to produce a suitable horticultural product. The slabs of base material can be shaped into the specialised forms of product such as propagating blocks, etc.

Characteristics of Rockwool

- It is very light weight (i.e. 70 kg per cubic metre).
- Most types of rockwool are approximately 5% solid material by volume. This leaves an enormous amount of space which can be filled by air, nutrients and water.
- Generally, it cannot be overwatered (there is

always adequate air space).

- The ratio of water to air in the average free draining slab is frequently two parts water to one part air.
- It takes longer to dry out than many other media, hence the chance of water stress is reduced.
- It is totally sterile. If it is to be reused, e.g. slabs in a soilless system, it may be sterilised with steam or chemicals, e.g. methyl bromide. It will withstand low pressure steam or steam/air treatment but not high temperature autoclaving which tends to break down the bonded structure.
- It has excellent insulation characteristics which keep the root zone from getting too hot or cold.
- The greater the depth of rockwool, the more air in proportion to water it will hold.
- Plants can continue to extract water from this medium even when it is only at 10 to 20% of its water-holding capacity. This is not so with other media. With most media, as the water is removed it becomes increasingly difficult for the remaining water to be extracted by the plant.
- If a rockwool slab does become over wet, excess water can be readily removed by tilting the slab for a short time.
- The water content (and hence the air content) of any piece of rockwool is influenced by the thickness of the material, the drainage characteristics of the surface upon which it stands, and the method of watering. For example, a 75 mm thick rockwool slab standing on polythene holds an average of 80% water and 17% air. The water content also varies through the thickness of the slab, starting from very wet at the base and getting drier with increasing height. The water in the rockwool is also only lightly bound and hence is readily available to the plant.
- It is chemically inert (except that it has a very small effect on pH).
- It doesn't affect the composition of nutrient formulas at all.
- It doesn't impede the availability of nutrients from solution at all.
- Cation exchange capacity is effectively zero and the material will not absorb or exchange nutrient ions from solution. One effect is that the material can be leached clean of any solution it contains.
- Biodegradability—Rockwool is a bonded form of natural rock fibres. Although it can be physically broken down by expanding roots or

by mechanical action, it is not biodegradable. It causes no environmental problems as it may easily be incorporated into the soil, where it should improve aeration and drainage.

- Rockwool has no long term pH buffer capacity, however, when nutrient solution is first added there may be an initial small pH rise. The rate and degree of reaction are dependent upon the pH and buffer capacity of the solution used to wet the rockwool.

Types of Rockwool

Rockwool can be obtained as preformed slabs or as loose flock or fibre material.

Slabs can vary in width, length and depth. Most manufacturers offer a variety of sizes.
- Small slabs partially cut into tiny cubes are used for propagation. Seeds or cuttings struck in these

Scented geranium cutting struck in a rockwool propagating block. (N.B. Plants need to be planted out before roots become so extensive. This cutting is less than 10 weeks old.)

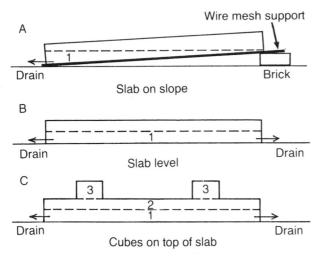

A Slab on slope

Wire mesh support

Drain   Brick

B Slab level

Drain   Drain

C Cubes on top of slab

Drain   Drain

1. Wettest area. Optimum conditions for most plants
2. Drier but still moist
3. Low water content

A or C are more suitable for plants which
prefer better aeration

Water levels in rockwool slabs. The slabs can be arranged to
suit individual plants' root aeration requirements. The depth of
water from the highest part of the rockwool to the lowest will
determine the overall wetness of the growing medium. A slab
on an angle, for instance, will hold a lower percentage of water
compared with air than one which is level.

blocks can be transferred to larger growing slabs
or blocks by carefully separating the individual
cubes and then planting them on or into the larger
slabs.
• Deeper slabs are commonly used to grow plants
which have a greater need for aeration, and
perhaps a preference for drier conditions.
• Shallower slabs may be used for plants requiring
more water.

Flock (i.e. loose rockwool) can be produced either
in a form which is water absorbent or a form which
repels water. It can also be obtained either as coarse,
medium or fine granules.
• Coarse flock has a greater water holding capacity
than fine flock.
• Flock can be used as a medium by itself, or
alternatively mixed with some other material.
• Absorbent types are used by themselves, water
repellent flock is generally mixed with other
materials to improve the structural
characteristics.
• Coarser grades of absorbent flock are more
commonly used in hydroponic beds. Finer grades
are used in propagation.

Applications for Slabs

Rockwool slabs are used for commercial production
of a large variety of horticultural crops in different
parts of the world. Some of the more important
rockwool slab grown crops are:

1. *Cut flowers:* carnations, chrysanthemums, roses,
gerberas.
2. *Vegetables:* tomatoes, capsicums, cucumbers, egg
plants, lettuces.

Applications for Flock

The following may be grown successfully in the
following grades of flock:

1. Coarse grade absorbent:
   Growing: cymbidium orchids.
   Propagating: cucumber seedlings.
2. Medium grade absorbent:
   Growing: begonias.
   Propagating: tomatoes, cucumbers.
3. Fine grade absorbent:
   Growing: cucumbers, melons, lettuce and
   tomatoes.
   Propagating: finer seeds and cuttings.
4. 50% medium absorbent with 50% medium non
   absorbent:
   Growing: gerberas, freesias, anthuriums and
   cymbidium orchids.

Problems of Rockwool

Algae can grow on the surface of rockwool. This
generally does not affect the crop, but over an
extended period of time may lead to an
impermeable layer developing which can stop water
penetrating the slab. Slabs are frequently wrapped
in white, grey or black plastic to stop light. Without
light, algae will not grow.

System Options and Design

The most commonly used system is where
propagated plants, such as vegetable seedlings, are
transferred into individual rockwool cubes (usually
75 mm) where they grow on until well established.
The cubes are then planted onto individually plastic
wrapped slabs of rockwool where cuts have been
made into the plastic. Slits are also made in the
plastic at the bottom of the slab to facilitate

Slab layout

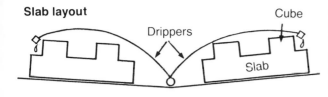

Dripper layout

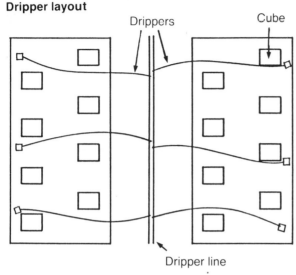

Dripper line

Arrangement of rockwool slabs.

drainage. Individual drippers are placed into each cube to supply nutrient solution. The excess solution runs out into a drain. This method is almost entirely operated as an open system.

Reusing Slabs

The cost of slabs is a significant component of production costs, particularly for single season crops. If the slab hasn't been penetrated too much by an invasive root system and the previous crops weren't seriously affected by major root diseases and pests then it can be sterilised and reused. There may be a gradual loss of slab height after slabs have been steam sterilised. This must be taken into consideration when deciding if it is worthwhile reusing the slabs.

Rockwool for Propagation

Rockwool propagation blocks are used to provide transplants for growing not only in rockwool systems, but also in aggregate culture and NFT. They are commonly made from a 40 mm thick slab of rockwool with horizontal fibres and slits from the top to give individual blocks 40 mm square.

Deeper propagation blocks are also available for propagating plants which require better drainage (i.e. the greater depth, hence greater head of water, increases aeration in those blocks).

The only problem which can occur with propagation blocks relates to them becoming too wet. This is a problem with some plant species if the blocks are not managed properly. They must be sat in or on a freely draining surface and rate of irrigations must be limited. Remember young seedlings or cuttings are more susceptible to poor conditions than established plants.

Australian Rockwool Propagating Blocks

Parts of the following sections on propagation are from a paper presented at the Australian Horticultural Correspondence School's 1985 Summer Update Conference by Mike Hartley of

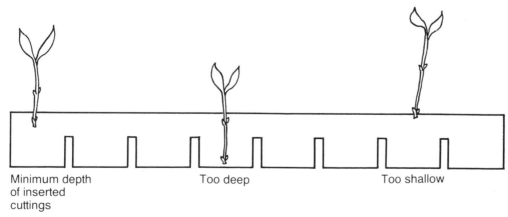

Minimum depth of inserted cuttings   Too deep   Too shallow

Striking cuttings in rockwool propagating blocks. The depth of inserted cuttings is dependant on anchorage and moisture surrounding the cutting.

CSR Ltd, manufacturers of Growool in Australia.

Standard propagating blocks Each block is 35 mm square and 40 mm high, 21 blocks per sheet; 3 sheets fit into the Australian standard size propagating tray.

The horizontal fibred blocks originally gave problems with separation and roots growing into adjacent blocks. Similar problems were observed on a visit to Europe, so an improved propagating block was developed which had vertical fibre orientation, and was grooved underneath. This type of block is less convenient to manufacture but has since proved to be very successful. Some advantages of this type of block are: roots grow vertically rather than mostly horizontally; the gap gives a degree of aerial pruning; and they are very easy to separate.

Sheet and block sizes A major advantage of rockwool propagating blocks is that they can be manufactured in sheets, with consequent convenience and time savings. However there needs to be a rational basis for selecting the sheet and block sizes. In Australia there is a standard nursery propagation tray which, while certainly not used universally, is very widely used. Consequently it was decided to size the propagating block sheet to fit this tray.

The dimensions of this tray are 280 × 340 mm. After experimenting, the most convenient size of sheet was found to be one that would fit 3 sheets to the tray. The corresponding sheet size was set at 266 × 110 mm, and 40 mm thick. This is grooved from underneath to give 3 rows of 7 individual blocks, i.e. 21 blocks per sheet, or 63 blocks per tray. The blocks are each 35 × 35 mm and 40 mm high. On top of each block is a hole which is mainly an indication of the location of the block underneath. The use of a vertical fibre format makes the diameter of the cutting less critical.

These blocks are packed in lots of 100 sheets, i.e. 2100 blocks, in a carton which weighs about 10 kg.

The original release was of only one height of block, namely 40 mm. This was suitable for propagating indoor plants and vegetables. However, when used for shrubs and Australian native plants it was less successful unless care was taken to increase aeration by reducing water content. This could also be achieved by increasing the height of the block. Consequently a 57 mm tall block was developed in the same 35 × 35 mm format as the standard 40 mm type. This tall block also suits long cuttings.

There was also a demand for smaller blocks giving more per tray. In this case a product was developed with the same sheet size and 40 mm height. The sheet is subdivided into 4 rows of 9 blocks, i.e. 36 blocks per sheet, or 108 blocks per tray. The individual blocks are 25 × 25 mm × 40 mm high.

Propagation Applications

Experimentation in Australia during the early 1980s led to commercial scale propagation, initially to supply the following plants for hydroponic crops:

• Tomatoes and cucumbers from seed
• Roses and carnations from cuttings.

These were very successful but highlighted important areas for further work. The rose cuttings needed control of the water content of the blocks and liquid feeding the vegetables showed that some commercial fertilisers are very low in iron and hence need supplementing with iron chelate. There were major problems with some single solution concentrated liquid fertilisers which precipitated calcium phosphate, leading to the development of deficiencies of both these elements.

In Australia commercial scale nursery propagation in rockwool was initiated by propagators who were having problems either with striking or transplanting. Examples of problem plants were *Grevillea* 'Robyn Gordon' and miniature roses. Both struck very well in rockwool and transplanting losses were effectively reduced to zero, although *Grevillea* 'Robyn Gordon' required careful management of the water content in order to give a reliable strike.

Although the initial incentive for using rockwool was to solve problems, once propagators were using the system they came to realise some of the other benefits involved. One such was Andrew Burton, who then integrated rockwool into his production system to make maximum use of its benefits and consequent labour cost savings.

Triggered by the need to supply soilless crop growers, several major specialist carnation and chrysanthemum propagators began propagating to order in rockwool.

A grower of tube stock commenced selling plants propagated in rockwool instead of by traditional methods in tubes. The change to propagation in

Nutrient solution runs from the collection pipe into a 'nutrient tank' (container) from where it is recycled to the tops of the channels. (Chapter 5)

Lettuce seedlings purchased in growplugs are planted into the hydroponic channels. (Chapter 5)

Marigolds in perlite, using a foam box. (Chapter 7)

Left: Wrapped rockwool slabs. (Chapter 6)

Vegetables in a scoria bed. (Chapter 7)

rockwool was unannounced, however, and there was some resistance from customers who did not know the material. He now advertises some lines as grown only in rockwool and provides most other lines in rockwool unless requested otherwise.

Horticultural rockwool was launched onto the Australian market in the early 1980s. By 1985 well over 300 different plant species had been successfully propagated in rockwool propagating blocks. The range of plants grown extends over flowers, indoor plants, vegetables, trees, shrubs and Australian native plants. Propagation has been initiated from a range of seeds, seedlings, tissue culture plants, hardwood and softwood cuttings.

The bulk of rockwool propagation to date has been of nursery plants from cuttings. These have then been potted on into conventional potting media. A major use has been the propagation of vegetables for growing on in the soil as well as in soilless systems, although use with soil has been limited to date. Large seeds such as cucumber, zucchini, melon, sweet corn, legumes, etc. are normally sown direct, whereas it is usually more convenient with smaller seeded vegetables to prick out seedlings into the blocks. Flower plants are propagated for growing cut flower crops, also for use in the soil as well as in soilless systems. When larger 'slippery' seeds are pushed into rockwool and then watered, they have a tendency to work their way out of the block to sit on the surface, which can expose them to drying out and severe stress. This does not happen with smaller seeds, or seeds with a rough seed coat.

When plants are intended to be grown on into a soilless system, they are often propagated directly into a rockwool wrapped cube. This is often cheaper and more convenient than propagating into a block and later transplanting into a wrapped cube which has a hole to take the block.

Propagation of Micro-cuttings from Tissue Culture

There has been considerable expansion in using rockwool for deflasking tissue cultured plants. It has proved to be a very compatible medium for this purpose and particularly in the case of micro-cuttings it enables good support of these very small plants.

Several trial shipments of plants using rockwool as the propagating and growing medium have been exported to countries where the import of soil and similar growing media is not permitted. This use could have considerable potential particularly because of the beneficial effect on plant quality.

Recommended Practices for Propagation

Because of its properties, the following principles need to be considered when using rockwool propagating blocks:

• Use a block size suitable for the plant you are propagating.

• It is desirable to place sheets of blocks in trays with an open mesh base. Trays with a less open base restrict the drainage. Moving blocks without the support of trays can increase the damage to plant roots. N.B. Trays can be washed in antiseptic and reused many times over.

• Thoroughly saturate blocks before using them. Preferably immerse in a tub of water or alternatively use overhead watering, but be thorough! Then allow to drain for several minutes before use.

• Practise a high level of cleanliness. Though rockwool is sterile when unpacked, disease can spread easily. The propagation area, greenhouse, tools and equipment (and the propagator's hands) should always be clean.

• Push seed into the block only as far as is needed to just cover it and keep it from drying out. Push a cutting in just far enough to keep it standing up. The bottom of the block is the wettest and the young plant shouldn't contact that part until it has started to grow. A seed or cutting without roots on it is more likely to rot if it gets too wet.

• Don't let the blocks get too wet.
—A deeper block will have a higher proportion of air to water.
—A block sitting on a bed of coarse sand will become drier than one sitting on a surface such as concrete or asbestos sheet.
—You can reduce the frequency of watering.
—Bottom heat can dry out the blocks faster than would otherwise be the case.
—Mist or fogging systems, or propagating in bell jars or a tent to raise humidity may be necessary for some plant varieties, but these techniques can also affect moisture levels in the propagation block.

• Most irrigation methods work well with rockwool, but each one will need to be used in a different way with respect to watering frequency.

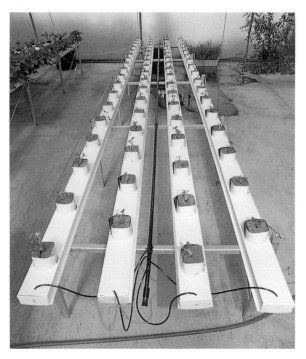

Rockwool cubes in NFT channel.

Rockwool propagation blocks, wrapped cubes and wrapped slab.

Tomatoes in rockwool.

Rockwool propagation blocks fit neatly into precut holes in wrapped cubes. Wrapped cubes sit on the surface of rockwool slabs.

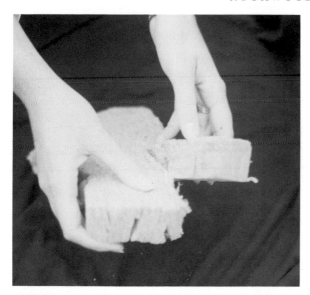

Rockwool propagating blocks should be torn lengthways when separating individual blocks.

• Transplant the propagated plant as soon as roots appear in the bottom of the block. Young plants do not 'hold' as well in rockwool propagation blocks as they do in tubes.

• Transplant into larger rockwool blocks or other media without removing rockwool from around the roots of the young plant. Carefully tear a strip of blocks from the slab and remove individual blocks from the strip one by one. Do not squeeze the cubes any more than you have to. Handle gently. This minimises root damage.

• If planting into a medium other than rockwool, recognise the differences between the two media and allow for those differences. If the medium you transplant into is more water absorbant than rockwool it can soak the moisture out of the rockwool block and dry it out before the roots begin to grow into the new medium. As most of the established roots are in the rockwool, they can be left suffering water stress. Once the roots establish into the new medium, problems such as this will disappear.

Benefits of Rockwool Propagation

Using rockwool for propagation can be of advantage to all types and sizes of nurseries. Some of the benefits to be obtained are as follows:

• A wide variety of plants strike faster in rockwool than in conventional media. This gives a quicker turnover in the nursery and hence more efficient use of propagation facilities.

• Plants propagated in rockwool can be transplanted as soon as the roots are emerging from the block, or even earlier in some circumstances. By comparison, in a tube the root system has to develop sufficiently to bind the medium together before it can be transplanted.

• Rockwool is lightweight and easier to move around the nursery.

• It is easier to insert cuttings into rockwool. Softwood cuttings which need a hole to be made, for instance, can be simply pushed into rockwool.

• Transplant shock can be less than with conventional media provided the block is handled carefully. The seedling doesn't need to be pricked out and the cutting doesn't need to be bare rooted from the propagating mix and planted into a tube.

• Overall propagation cost is often less than with conventional media largely due to savings on labour costs. Time and motion studies have shown that the total time involved per plant for propagating in rockwool is less than for propagating in a

Strawberry plants growing in individual Growool rockwool pieces in a 110 mm diameter plastic pipe. The plants are intermittently fed by a recirculating solution.

conventional mix and potting into a tube. (N.B. Rockwool propagation has only one stage before planting out into the hydroponic system. Conventional methods have two stages—striking the seed or cutting, then planting into a tube or seedling tray/punnet.)

The difference in strike and germination rates and time between a conventional peat:perlite mix (1:1) and rockwool

(Estimates based on work by staff of the Australian Horticultural Correspondence School, and paper presented by Mike Hartley of CSR as mentioned earlier.)

These figures relate to Melbourne, Victoria.

Item	Rockwool		Peat:perlite	
	Days	%	Days	%
Aeschynanthus sp. (cuttings)	20	90	26	90
Aphelandra sp. (cuttings)	19	100	19	95
Begonia (cuttings)	14	100	14–17	100
Bougainvillea (cuttings)	22	70–90	28	60–80
Carnation (seed)	2	—	7	—
Clerodendron (cuttings)	9	100	15	80
Coleus (cuttings)	5	100	7–10	100
Fittonia (cuttings)	13	100	14	100
Ficus (cuttings)	18–20	90	22–24	90
Hoya carnosa (cuttings)	10–11	100	13–17	95
Lonicera nitida (cuttings)	14	100	20–25	95
Maranta (cuttings)	13	100	18–20	100
Marigold (seed)	4	—	6–10	—
Pelargonium (cuttings)	6–10	100	8–15	100
Peperomia (cuttings)	22	100	19	100
Rose—miniature (cuttings)	20–30	95	25–35	95
Syngonium sp. (cuttings)	16	100	25	100

Comparison of costs of plants propagated in rockwool and conventional tube-mix (Australian cents per plant)

From talk by M. Hartley, CSR Australia, at AHCS Summer Update Conference, 1985.

Component	Rockwool	Tube + mix
Material	1.6	1.3
Labour (inc. potting and recycling tubes)	2.6	5.1
Cost of slower turnaround of propagating space	nil	0.8
Cost of mixing and storing propagating medium	nil	0.8
Total	4.2	8.0

These figures assume plant densities and losses are the same in Growool as in conventional sand peat mixes, which in fact is not necessarily the case. In practice there are further cost benefits with rockwool over conventional media.

Limitations Experienced in the Use of Rockwool Propagating Blocks

These limitations are cited from Australian experiences, and many have been overcome as growers become more familiar with the products and their properties.

• There will obviously be cuttings which are too large for standard propagation blocks. If they are forced into the blocks these tend to split. 'Dibbing' can help, otherwise a larger block or wrapped cube should be used.

Part of the root system of a tomato plant growing in a slab of rockwool.

A sheet of rockwool propagating blocks ready to be torn apart for transplanting of carnations.

Growing on of carnation plants in wrapped cubes before planting out for cropping.

Transplanting propagated carnation into rockwool 75 mm wrapped cube for growing on.

• Propagating blocks are rarely suitable for holding plants for extended periods once they have rooted. If plants are fed as they need to be, then their roots will eventually grow into the adjoining blocks. This makes them difficult to separate and will cause root damage at that time. A tendency to damping off has been reported for some plants held for long periods, although in some cases additional drainage has helped. The material certainly gives optimum results if cuttings are transplanted soon after striking.

Advanced carnation plant in 75 mm wrapped cube being planted out onto a rockwool slab.

• Transplanting rockwool blocks into soil may result in failure if the soil has a high draining capacity. Because the water in the rockwool is only lightly bound, it can be drained away before the plant roots have grown into the soil. Consequently care must be taken to keep the blocks moist after planting. This may require mulching and regular watering.

Young carnation crop growing on in rockwool slabs. The layout of two rows of slabs along the bed with a gap in between is designed to help air movement through the crop.

7 Aggregate Culture

Aggregate culture involves growing in a material made up of loose particles held in some type of container.

The most commonly used aggregate materials in commercial hydroponics are sand, perlite and gravel. Gravel differs from sand in that the particles are larger, however, sand and gravel culture are in many instances interchangeable terms. Sawdust culture is also of some commercial significance in Canada and South Africa.

Alternatives for Containers

1. Greenhouse floor

Here the entire floor of a greenhouse may be covered with sand or some other aggregate. The surface below the media must be first graded to produce slopes which will give appropriate drainage to a collection point from where solution can either be recirculated or disposed of. The graded surface must be covered with a material which will keep the media clean. It may be concreted or covered with asphalt (N.B. asphalt is cheaper than concrete); or covered with heavy duty PVC film laid on a bed of fine sand.

2. Bag culture

Plastic bags are an inexpensive container, usually used with drippers into each bag. These bags will generally break down with exposure to light and are not suitable for permanent crops (over several years).

3. Polystyrene boxes

Polystyrene boxes, commonly used for packing fruit, have been used successfully by many commercial growers for holding aggregate.

4. Raised beds

Generally a concrete slab is laid first, with a slope to allow drainage to a collection point at one end of the system. Walls can then be constructed from brick, stone or concrete. The bed is then filled with media.

N.B. Fresh concrete will affect the pH and calcium levels in your media. It is necessary for concrete to be left and washed periodically for at least several weeks before using it.

5. Fibreglass and plastics

Fibreglass and rigid plastics are excellent for constructing aggregate beds, and have real value for hobby systems. Cost limits their application in commercial situations though.

6. Metal

Galvanised metal troughs have been successful provided they are painted to stop nutrient solution reacting with the galvanising.

7. Flexible liners

Flexible polythene film or swimming pool and agricultural dam lining materials can be used to line beds built with timber, bricks, concrete or formed earth.

Aggregate bed growing a variety of vegetables.

1. A bed is flooded, with a tap or valve on the drainage outlet being closed, and then the valve is opened and excess solution drained off.

2. Nutrient solution is fed into the top of a bed which has a sloping base below the media. A film of solution flows across the bottom of the bed, below the media. Solution moves up into the media at all points, by capillary action. Excess solution may drain into a sump and be recirculated.

3. Nutrient solution is fed into the media via wicks from a tank containing solution below the beds or containers.

4. Containers (e.g. pots or foam trays) containing media are sat in a tray (sometimes on top of capillary matting). The tray is periodically flooded with nutrient solution which rises into the containers via capillary action.

Surface Irrigation

The most popular way to supply nutrient to the surface of aggregate media is by trickle or drip irrigation.

Surface irrigation may alternatively use sprayers, however that method will wet foliage and perhaps fruits or flowers, which in turn can promote fungal diseases or lead to other types of damage to the plants.

Alternatives for Delivering Nutrient Solution

Nutrient solution can be applied to aggregate culture either on the surface of the media, or from below the media.

Sub-surface Irrigation

If nutrient is applied from underneath, the media must normally have the ability to carry solution via capillary action upwards. This may not work for such media as coarse sand or gravel, and it will not work for many of the plastic materials.

Perlite, rockwool, vermiculite and peat all have adequate capillary action characteristics to work with sub-surface irrigation.

Sub-surface irrigation can operate in the following ways:

Irrigation Frequency

The frequency of irrigations is influenced by the following characteristics of an aggregate:

1. Particle shape and porosity
Aggregate particles which have a regular (e.g. ball-like) shape and a smooth surface require more frequent irrigations. If the particles have crevices in their surface or are porous (i.e. water absorbant), the frequency of irrigations will be less.

2. Particle size
Large particles require more frequent irrigations than smaller particles.

3. Plant requirements and tolerances
Plants which tolerate greater variation in water levels can be irrigated heavily and left longer before a further irrigation. Plants which are less tolerant of such variations must be watered less, but more

Chrysanthemums in raised brick beds, using gravel culture.

frequently to keep moisture levels within a narrower range of tolerance.

4. Climatic factors

Water is lost at a faster rate through evaporation in windy or hot conditions, or in systems which have water more exposed to the air.

Irrigation and Nutrition

A system which is irrigated less frequently has a lower moisture content in the media just before each irrigation than one which is irrigated more often. When the moisture content is lower, the EC or nutrient salt concentration increases. (i.e. The plant has been extracting water and useable nutrients from the media but leaving behind salt residues—the unusable parts of the nutrients. These salt residues when added to the normal nutrient solution which is left create a more concentrated solution than what was first applied. A further factor is the loss of moisture from the aggregate surface through evaporation. The water which evaporates from the aggregate surface leaves its share of the original nutrient in the media, raising the concentration further.)

Plants which are less tolerant of high EC levels are perhaps better grown in medium which is suited to more frequent irrigations, and treated that way to minimise the EC creeping up between irrigations.

Sometimes nutrient solution is heated to warm the root zone and produce better growth. There is a danger if the solution is overheated. At a higher temperature, the solubility of nutrient salts, and effectively the EC, will increase. This can upset the delicate balance of the nutrient solution, and may in extreme situations cause nutrient burn to the roots of particularly susceptible plants.

Collecting Run-off

Excess nutrient solution must be collected at the lower end of an aggregate bed or at the bottom of a container and disposed of. Some of the ways this can be done are:

Flume

An open channel at the end of a bed which takes excess solution to a sump for recycling or disposal. The difficulty with a flume is that being exposed to the air, algae can grow in the channel and foreign matter such as twigs or leaves can fall in. Without a good filtration system and regular cleaning, this can lead to the water flow becoming blocked.

Collection pipe

Here a pipe collects excess water and conveys it to the sump. Being sealed, the pipe doesn't have the same problems as a flume. Do not use clear (see-through pipe though, which will allow algae to grow in it.

Gravel surface and sub-surface drain

Systems which use bags or foam boxes fed with drippers often run the excess nutrient solution to waste. In such systems it is important to maintain a dry and clean surface below the container. To do this the surface must be either sealed or covered with a coarse, freely draining gravel on top of a well-draining soil. In clay soils it is advisable to install sub-surface agricultural drainage pipes to remove waste solution from the growing area.

Sculpted concrete floor

A sealed surface under beds can be sloped so that solution will drain into a collection pit (or pits). N.B. Be careful where you dispose of waste solution. You can build up significant salt levels at your disposal point creating very real problems with the soil in that area. If salt levels become too high even weeds will not grow, and erosion could become a problem.

The Media

Gravel

Particles usually vary between 3 and 15 mm diameter. Crushed granitic rock or porous volcanic rock (e.g. scoria) are the most commonly used materials. More than 50% of the particles should be less than 1 cm in diameter, and there should be no dust or fine particles less than 1 mm diameter (this fine material should be washed out before use).

Calcareous rock (e.g. limestone) should not be used because it will create pH shifts. This type of rock also adds calcium and magnesium to the solution. If calcareous rock must be used, pH must be monitored and regularly adjusted; and calcium/magnesium levels must be lowered in the nutrient solution.

Fresh scoria has a high pH, but if weathered before use will drop to an acceptable level.

Perlite and coarse sand media.

Coarse granitic sand.

Scoria.

Fired shale has been used for some hydroponics, however due to its porous nature, salt residues tend to build up to toxic levels in the rock and are difficult to leach out after a few years. Porous rock can crumble over time and is generally unsuitable for commercial systems.

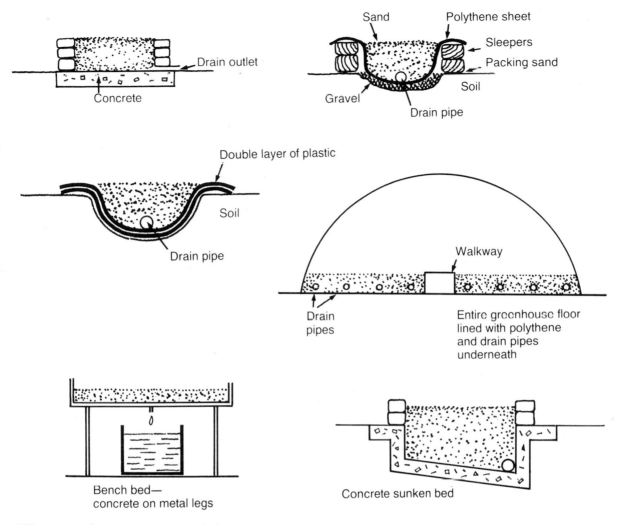

Different ways of constructing aggregate beds.

Sand

Sand culture can use particles less than 1 mm in diameter; if the particles are too fine however, the system can become waterlogged.

Sand should be washed to remove chemical impurities and dust particles, and screened to ensure uniform particle sizes, before being used in hydroponics.

Beach sand has been used successfully in some places (e.g. installations in the Middle East), but only after thorough washing to remove salt. If beach sand is used, it should be chemically tested after washing and before using. Silica, quartz or granitic sands are best.

It is rare that sand is calcareous, however, be aware that calcareous sands are not generally suitable for hydroponics. (N.B. Sand containing large amounts of shell grit may be a problem.)

Additives

Perlite, peat, sawdust, vermiculite or rockwool fibre may be added to sand or gravel to increase the water-holding capacity where a crop requiring more moisture is being grown.

Ausperl Perlite Grobag System

Perlite is available from various suppliers around the world, prewrapped in polythene. Bags are

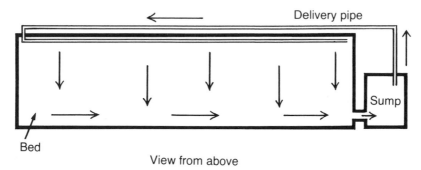

Delivery pipe

Sump

Bed

View from above

Solution drips from this pipe

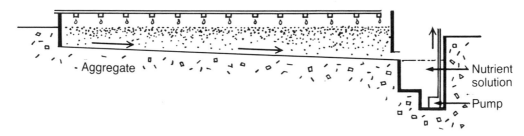

- Aggregate

Nutrient solution

Pump

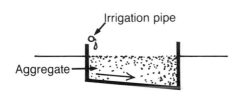

Irrigation pipe

Aggregate

End view

Recirculating aggregate culture bed. Above, side and end view, with arrows indicating the direction of nutrient flow.

commonly 25 litre size. As with wrapped rockwool slabs, a slit can be cut into the plastic wherever a plant is to be inserted, drainage holes cut in the bottom of the bag and nutrient solution applied through a drip irrigation system.

Ausperl Grobags are an Australian product available from Australian Perlite, 22 McPherson St, Banksmeadow, NSW, 2019.

Setting Up the System

Ausperl bags should be used under sterile conditions to prevent soil-borne diseases contaminating the perlite. All soil should be sterilised before entering the greenhouse, surrounding weeds should be cleared and greenhouse floors should be covered with white polythene sheeting before setting up the system.

When setting up the system, the bags should be laid end to end, ideally in double rows. They are often slightly raised, using polystyrene, to allow placement of root-zone heating pipes. Each bag should have a minimum of three drippers which are connected to the feeder line. Each double row should have a drainage furrow placed in the middle.

The bags should be prepared in the following way:

- Cut holes in the top of the bag and insert drippers.
- Cut one or two horizontal drainage slits to a length of 4 cm, usually 20 mm from the base of the bag (see below). The slits should be made on the side of the drainage furrow.
- Pump nutrient slowly into the bag until the perlite is moist and the solution is draining out of the slits. The perlite will be moist enough once moisture can be squeezed out of individual grains.
- Cut holes in bags and place plants in the perlite at the same level as for ground growing.

Using the System

Perlite has a very strong capillary action which ensures that nutrients are drawn upwards from the reservoir at the base of the bag. The reservoir maintains root moisture at an optimum level, therefore the reservoir should never be allowed to dry out. Excess nutrient solution runs to waste, so the perlite never becomes too wet.

The depth of the reservoir is determined by the medium the crop is propagated in. Plants propagated in perlite, vermiculite or peat should have slits cut 20 mm from the bottom of the bag. Plants propagated in rockwool blocks require an

Vermiculite.

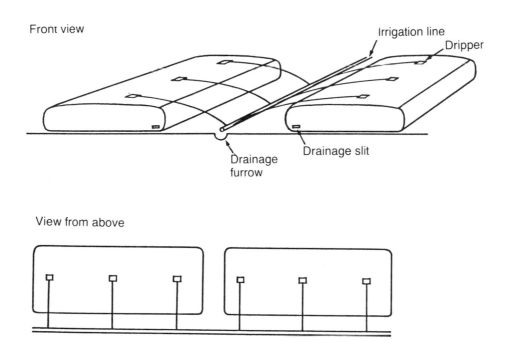

Ausperl perlite Grobags system. Bags are set in double rows with a central drainage furrow and irrigation line. A minimum of three drippers should be placed at each bag.

initial slit to be made 75 mm from the bottom to prevent too much water being drawn from the block. Once roots are established (usually within 2 weeks), the slits can be lowered to the normal 20 mm height.

With good quality water, 10% of the solution should be run to waste. EC levels should be checked regularly; if they increase above set limits more solution should be run to waste at each feed. If the solution EC still does not decrease, the EC of the input solution should be reduced (not more than 0.5 mS/cm). Flushing should only be done with dilute solution, not water, as the roots cannot tolerate the sudden change in solution concentration.

8   Other Techniques—Selected Examples

Wick Systems

A wick system uses a cord or fibrous piece of material which has the ability to absorb nutrient solution and raise it upwards by capillary action. Capillary action is the force which makes liquid travel upwards against the force of gravity. This is the same force which causes liquid parrafin to soak up a wick in a paraffin lamp and supply fuel from the bottom to the fire burning at the top.

A typical wick system involves the supply of nutrient solution to an aggregate bed from a reservoir of nutrient solution below the bed. Another method uses pots standing in a tray of nutrient solution. Here a wick material such as rockwool can be pushed through the drainage holes in the base of the pot so that some goes into the pot and some hangs out of the bottom. The pots are filled with a medium such as sand, and then planted. The trough is supplied with nutrient solution which soaks up the wick to moisten the sand.

Bag Culture

Plastic bags with drainage holes are used to hold hydroponic media. Nutrients are supplied by a trickle or drip irrigation system outlet to the top of each bag. Drainage holes at the bottom of the bag allow any excess to drain away. This system is not a recirculating system—nutrient solution is run to waste. Normally only one plant is grown in each bag, and bags are spaced at intervals according to the requirements of the plant variety being grown.

The bags will need flushing periodically to remove salt residues which could otherwise build to toxic levels.

Bags must sit on top of a surface which drains freely and remains relatively dry so that roots do not grow out through the holes in the bottom of the bag. They should never sit on top of soil. In America bags are often sat on plastic sheet. They can also sit on coarse gravel, a sealed surface such as asphalt or concrete, or on a couple of bricks. Bag culture is used commercially in many countries including parts of North America. The major advantage of this technique is its establishment cost. It is perhaps one of the least expensive methods to set up.

Column Culture

This involves growing plants in vertical tubes with slits or holes cut in the sides for plants to grow from. Nutrient solution can be applied to the top and allowed to filter through the medium to the bottom from where it can be either run to waste or collected and recirculated. The principal advantage is to get more plants in a specified area. A disadvantage is the effect of gravity which can result in lower sections of the medium being wetter (due to the weight of water above). This system is not generally used for commercial growing.

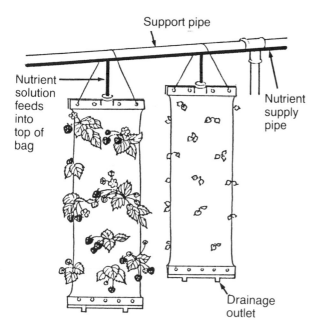

Column culture in hanging bags is useful for growing plants where space is restricted. Bags are normally made from plastics or other synthetic materials. Media in these bags need to be light weight—perlite or rockwool fibre is appropriate, gravel or sand is not. Columns may also be made with rigid materials such as PVC pipe.

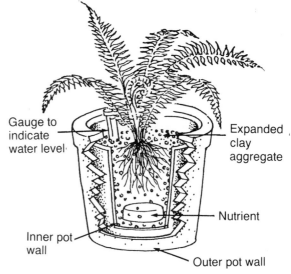

Luwasa pot. Primarily used for home gardening of indoor plants. The system is available as a kit, including decorative pot, aggregate, nutrients and instructions.

Luwasa

Luwasa is a European company which produces pots fed by capillary action via a store of nutrient solution held in a reservoir below the medium. Expanded clay aggregate is used as the medium. The Luwasa systems are sold as a kit, with a decorative plastic pot and built in reservoir, a pack of aggregate, a supply of nutrients and instructions. They are promoted for growing indoor plants in the home.

This system has some application for commercial interior plantscaping, but is not appropriate for crop production.

American Sawdust Culture

Sawdust culture is a hydroponic method practised by growers on a commercial scale in various parts of North America, principally on the west coast of Canada and the USA where there is a significant forest industry and ample, cheap supplies of sawdust as a growing medium.

In these areas sawdust culture is practised in greenhouse growing, either using beds or bag culture. The best wood sources have been *Pseudotsuga menziesii* (Douglas fir) and *Tsuga heterophylla* (western hemlock). *Thuja plicata* sawdust is toxic and should not be used.

Beds are commonly built as follows:

1. The ground surface is sculpted to form a channel with a slope along its length and a 'U' or 'V' shape in cross-section.
2. Timber slabs are fixed on the edges of the depression.
3. Plastic sheet (or something similar) is laid into the pit and fixed to the tops of the timber walls.
4. A 5 cm drainage pipe is run along the length of the pit/bed on top of the plastic.
5. The pit is then filled to a depth of 25–30 cm with sawdust.

Because sawdust has a good cation exchange capacity, nutrient solution has been applied successfully in a rather unconventional way. Before filling the bed with sawdust, the nutrient is mixed into the sawdust. After that the crop is irrigated with a different nutrient formulation, supplying only nitrogen and potassium. Sufficient micronutrients, calcium, phosphorus and magnesium will remain in the sawdust to supply the crop needs until harvest.

Alternatively, nutrient can be applied as with other hydroponic systems, a full nutrient solution with every irrigation.

There is a real danger of salt build-up to toxic levels in sawdust culture. Conductivity (EC) readings need to be taken regularly, and for most crops, at levels of 4.0 mS/cm or higher, the system needs to be leached through with water.

Peat Culture

The Bently system

Reference: Maxwell Bently, *Hydroponics Plus*, O'Connor Printers, 3600 South Duluth Ave, Sioux Falls, Sth Dakota, USA, 1974.

Dr Bently, a pharmacologist, puts forward his own system of hydroponics in this book, based on experience which goes back to his first experiments with hydroponics in 1942.

This system is based on three ideas:

1. The container as the basic growth unit
He advocates an above ground, sterilised container. Initially he used polythene bags, which were cheap and effective (30 × 45 cm and 8 ml black polythene). More recently he has used standard black plastic pots, 2 gallon buckets or larger.

2. The growing medium
He has used a mix of vermiculite with peat moss, coarse river sand and charcoal.

4 × 4 cubic ft bales of vermiculite
1 × 12 cubic ft bale peat moss
8 cubic ft (2 wheelbarrows) of coarse river sand
4 cubic ft of charcoal

To this he adds 6.8 kg (15 lb) of agricultural gypsum and 1.8 kg (4 lb) of triple superphosphate and mixes thoroughly dry.

He then uses the following chemical nutrient solution:

77 litres (16 gallons) of water mixed with
1.8 kg (4 lb) potassium nitrate

Column culture of strawberries.

450 g (1 lb) epsom salts
60 g (2 oz) Sequestrene (provides iron)
30 g (1 oz) borax (be careful—more borax can cause boron toxicity)

The solution should be bright red when well dissolved.

3. The role of irrigation
A trickle irrigation system provides a constant flow of nutrient solution.

The major disadvantages of the peat are:

1. It frequently has a low pH (often around pH 4.5).
2. It has a high cation exchange capacity (i.e. ability to hold nutrients). This can result in salt build-up and toxicities.
3. In its raw state it will inevitably have nutrients in it due to the high cation exchange capacity. These nutrients interfere with the balance of the nutrient solution.

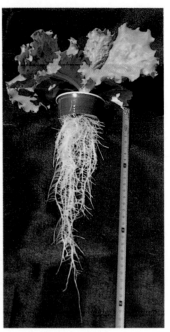

Three weeks after transplanting, lettuce plant which has been grown in aeroponic system has extensive, healthy root system. (Chapter 8)

Aeroponic growing bench, showing root chamber and curved plastic bench top. (Chapter 8)

Polythene film house—grape growing hydroponically in tub. (Chapter 10)

Overhead sprinkler system on NFT is used for cooling. (Chapter 10)

Shading and artificial lighting used to bring chrysanthemums into flower out of season. Shading with blankets drawn over metal frames. (Chapter 10)

The 'Ultimate' Hydroponic System— Aeroponics

K. Maxwell MSc. Agr., JP
World Councillor and Aust. Rep. ISOSC

The International Society for Soilless Culture in their classification of systems and methods of soilless culture (Steiner, A. A. 1976) defined aeroponics as 'The system where the roots are continuously or discontinuously in an environment saturated with fine drops (a mist or aerosol) of nutrient solution'.

Many thinking people, world-wide, consider the future of successful crop production lies in a universal cropping system in which water and fertilisers can be used efficiently. Perhaps aeroponics is the answer? This type of culture is widely used in laboratory studies in plant physiology because of the unique opportunities for studying plant growth and development.

Practical applications in the field have not been commercially demonstrated, except on a very limited scale in Italy and Israel. Complexity of design, costs, and maintenance requirements have been considered to be the primary factors against wider acceptance compared to other hydroponic systems.

Many researchers consider that only 'true hydroponics' (that is, using bare-rooted plants) gives the grower full control over the root parameters and thereby a possibility of optimising the growth of plants compared to solid substrate culture.

Aeroponic systems differ from other hydroponic systems in two main ways. Firstly no inert medium is required and secondly the nutrient solution is provided by direct sprinkling to the roots.

The first aeroponic system was evolved at the University of Pia in Italy by Dr Massantini. This lead in the 1960s to the development of the 'colonna di coltura'. This consisted of an aeroponic pipe supporting three relatively small cultivation trays fitted with sprinklers and covered with polystyrene lids. A range of plants was grown quite successfully but it was expensive.

Technical Aspects

1. Aeration

The importance of an adequate supply of oxygen to plant roots, particularly in water culture, has been well established. Depletion of oxygen will have an adverse effect on cropping.

Over 50% of the dry weight of the plant is made up of oxygen. Much of it is taken up directly from the air through the leaves *but* an important part comes from the oxygen dissolved in the water around the roots. If this supply of oxygen is diminished or cut off the plant will die.

The only practical way in which oxygen can enter the water is by diffusion and this can be assisted by mechanical methods which increase the water surface area. In general aeroponic misting has no problem with oxygen deficiency, but with high pressure aeroponic systems it is technically impossible to keep the atomising nozzles clean; also these systems have high energy costs to operate. Another problem is that with plants having big root systems, such as tomatoes and cucumbers, a large and expensive 'root chamber' is needed.

In order to have a perfect exchange of oxygen a loose root system is needed together with adequate water.

2. Water Supply

Any system of agriculture is limited by the quality of the water and this is especially important with hydroponics.

In general, any drinking water can be used, but brackish or very 'hard' water should be avoided. If there is any doubt a water analysis should be arranged.

The use of dam water for hydroponics is not recommended because of the commonly present *Pithium* and *Fusarium* fungi which can cause disease problems. If such water is used it must be freed from these fungi either physically through filtration or chemically.

Today there are many hydroponic techniques, which often makes it difficult for the grower to decide on what is the best to experiment with before making the final decision. In general with the increasing knowledge available the systems tend to be more technical and thus expensive.

So it is very refreshing to see emerging in Australia a successful but simple system developed by Mr Keith Schwalbach, RMB 267 Singleton Road, Wilberforce, 2756—phone (045) 76 3227. Now one has the opportunity to start hydroponics, the 'plant growing revolution' of the 21st century, in a very inexpensive and technically simple way.

□ = planting holes   × = misting jets

Aeroponics. Top view of bench top showing arrangement of 48 planting holes and 8 misting jets.

The Schwalbach System

The following is an outline of the hydroponic system developed by Mr Schwalbach of Wilberforce, NSW.

Mr Schwalbach developed a back problem in early 1988 but wanted to continue with a more suitable hydroponic system than the more physically intensive sand-bed culture presently used. The new system should be simple but successful, as free from plant growing problems as possible and inexpensive.

After some reading and a chance comment from Keith Maxwell that 'perhaps aeroponics could be considered the ultimate system', the Schwalbach system was started and developed, perhaps for the first time, in Australia.

The essentials of the Schwalbach system are:

1. Water supply The water used came from an earth dam where there was no special provision to prevent contamination. This was the only water available and had to be used despite adverse comments in general for this type of water supply. The water was tested by the NSW Department of

A modern aeroponics setup contrasts with the older sand culture system.

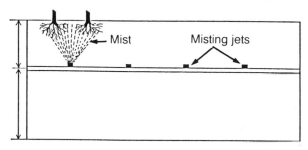

Aeroponics. Side view showing arrangement of misting jets.

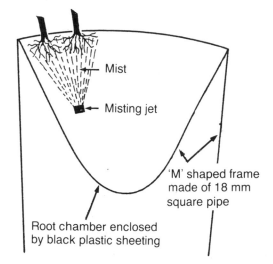

'M' shaped frame made of 18 mm square pipe

Root chamber enclosed by black plastic sheeting

Aeroponics. End view showing root chamber and arrangement of misting jets.

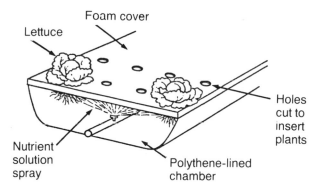

Lettuces growing in an aeroponics system.

Agriculture and found to be suitable for hydroponics and general farm use, including livestock.

The water was piped to a 200 litre plastic tank in which the nutrients were mixed.

2. Nutrient A general purpose ready-mixed nutrient was used, supplied by Simple Grow, Unit

28/132 Hassell Street, Wetherill Park, Australia 2164—phone (02) 604 0469.

3. Nutrient tank The nutrient solution was then transferred to the 200 litre plastic nutrient tank to which the circulatory pump was connected.

4. Pump The pump used was a Mono, quarter horse power, slow-revving pump which proved to be capable of servicing approximately 60 jets and was still able to by-pass some unwanted pressure back to the drum. The desired pressure required was about 100 kpa. Each jet needs to deliver approximately 10 litres per hour. Because pumps are expensive and critical it is recommended that a pump expert be consulted.

5. Growing benches
(i) Bench top The design has many desirable features. In the early stages marine plywood tops were used but found to be unsuitable. RELN Plastics were consulted, resulting in the adoption of structural foam polypropylene which has good rigidity. This type of plastic has many advantages as it is acid and alkaline resistant, tolerates a wide range of temperatures, is totally UV stabilised and totally 'food compatible'. The expected life of this plastic top compares well with that of other types, both because of the above properties and the thickness of 6 mm. These plastics are manufactured by RELN Plastics Pty Ltd, 11 Pembury Road, Minto, Australia 2566—phone (02) 603 2544.

The tops are curved to allow rain water to run off quickly, keeping them as dry as possible and almost eliminating nutrient dilution. The concave undersurface allows for a better trajectory of the spray, and the curvature gives greater strength. They are designed with pockets to take hoops so a mini-igloo or shade-cloth can be easily erected. The tops are interlocking and channelled so nutrient remains in the root chamber.

(ii) Root chamber The frame was made from 18 mm square galvanised pipe. The cladding of the root chamber was 2 metre wide black PVC plastic sheeting.

6. Misting apparatus The nutrient was fed off into each root chamber by a 13 mm black PVC pipe and jets were inserted in the appropriate places, preferably with a cut-off valve before each enters the chamber to facilitate servicing. The run-off nutrient gravitated back to the nutrient pump tank. The jets used were Wingfield misters RMST, capable of using 21 litres per hour at 22 PSI. In the Schwalbach system the pressure was reduced to 12 to 14 PSI delivering approximately 11 litres per hour per jet. This resulted in the optimum trajectory and gave the most desirable spray, and also allowed more jets to be serviced by an individual pump.

7. Growing routine Healthy seedlings with their small roots protruding are placed in the holes in the bench tops. If extreme weather is expected an appropriate cover could be drawn over the hoops of the mini-igloo to improve the micro-environment at very minimum cost. Within a day or two the all-important healthy 'water roots' will have developed, matched by an equally healthy top growth.

Plants can easily be relocated at any stage of their growth or left until the root growth becomes too extensive.

A characteristic of the aeroponic system is the astonishing growth rate of the root systems and the crops, e.g. lettuce roots measured 400 mm after 21 days, 700 mm after 35 days and at maturity, 42 days, measured in excess of 1000 mm. Tomato roots measured more than 2 m after 74 days.

Other observations made by Mr and Mrs Schwalbach which illustrate the success of this rather simple system include lettuce variety Imperial which, at maturity, measured 60 cm to 69 cm across the outer leaves and 23 cm to 26 cm across the very firm heart. Another example was the egg-shaped type tomato which yielded more than 20 kg of good quality fruit during its 28 weeks growth cycle. Other vegetables grown successfully to date include parsley, silverbeet, celery, cabbage, blue lake stringless beans, strawberries, mignonette and other fancy lettuce. As an experiment miniature water melons and rock melons and a few species of flowers all grew extremely well.

In the relatively short period since the development of this exciting aeroponic system a range of extremely healthy (despite using dam water) good quality vegetables were produced. The growth cycles, in general, were much shorter than for similar crops grown in soil.

The author would appreciate any comments concerning the aeroponic system of hydroponics.

9 Hydroponics Equipment

Irrigation Equipment

Nutrient solution can be applied in many different ways to a hydroponic system. It may be fed into the top of the media via an irrigation line or into the bottom of the media via absorbant wicks; it may also be supplied by flooding and draining off the excess, or by a continuous or intermittent flow through the bottom of the root zone.

Once applied, excess nutrient can be allowed to be lost or collected and recirculated through the system.

There are no hard and fast rules, and the best method may be different in any given situation.

Pumps

Pumps are used in hydroponics for moving nutrient solution through the system.

There are two main types of pump which can be used for irrigation systems:

1. Centrifugal pumps These operate through water being forced along driving propellors which are attached to a rotating shaft. This force creates pressure as water flows out to the discharge pipes. They are usually located above the water source. Water enters the pump through a suction pipe. The pump must be primed to remove air bubbles in the suction pipe.

2. Turbine pumps These work by water rotating a driving propellor inside a bowl which creates the water pressure. Vertical turbine pumps draw water

from a water surface. Submersible turbine pumps have the motor located below the pump in a well.

Pumps which are used for fertilising are known as positive displacement pump injectors. These injectors automatically add the correct amount of nutrient solution to the main supply line during irrigation.

Pumps used in hydroponics must be:

1. Non corrosive If nutrient solution contacts metal parts it can corrode and block irrigation lines.
2. Reliable Breakdowns (particularly in recirculating systems such as NFT) can result in serious crop losses.
3. Powerful Do not even come near to overloading a pump. Always buy something a little more powerful, operating at its maximum workload, than you will need.

Dripper Systems

Drip irrigation is perhaps the most popular way of supplying nutrient solution to commercial hydroponic systems using rockwool or aggregate. Drip systems supply water in a steady slow trickle to the base of each plant. This ensures that each plant is receiving a uniform supply of water at optimum levels for plant growth. It also means that the system is very water efficient.

The system is based on the construction of a main supply line of PVC pipes (e.g. 3–5 cm diam) which are connected to lateral feed lines (e.g. 2–2.5 cm diam). The individual drippers are attached to 1

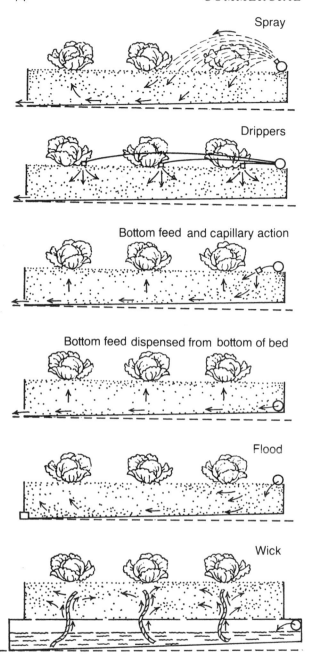

Different ways of applying nutrient solution.

Different types of drippers.

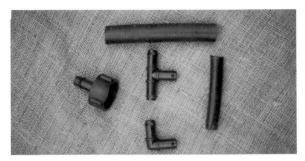

Drip irrigation pipe and connectors.

Dripper on sand bed.

cm flexible polyethylene pipes which come off the feed lines. Each irrigation takes several hours, using low water pressure (100 kpa). Microjets, which release a much larger volume of water in a shorter period of time, can be used as an alternative means of emitting solution. Drippers are prone to blockage through build-up of algae and sediments. Filters will reduce this problem, and careful management of your nutrient solutions will minimise precipitation of low solubility chemicals.

The major consideration with dripper systems is that every dripper operates at the same rate and therefore supplies equal amounts of nutrients to each plant. This should be achieved by correct layout of pumps, main and distribution lines. In situations where this may be difficult to achieve, it is possible to compensate by putting in more drippers per unit area to places with reduced flow rates. Irrigation lines and drippers should be cleaned between crops using acid solutions, according to manufacturer's suggestions.

An EC meter which measures the total salts concentration in the nutrient solution.

Solenoid Valves

A solenoid valve is a valve which can be opened and closed by using an electric signal. A solenoid can be installed to operate as a tap connecting a tank holding nutrient solution into the irrigation line. An EC meter in the irrigation line may, for instance, determine that nutrient levels have dropped too low, and then transmit a signal opening the solenoid and releasing concentrated nutrient. As the nutrient concentration rises in the irrigation line, the EC meter detects the change and at a given point will shut off the solenoid stopping any further release of nutrient. This is of course only one example of how a solenoid might be used in hydroponics.

Salinity Controllers

Total salts concentration is determined by measuring electrical conductivity of the nutrient solution. This needs to be monitored closely as the nutrient concentration will be continually dropping due to nutrients being taken out and used by the plants growing in the system. An EC meter (electroconductivity meter) is a device which measures the flow of electricity between two electrodes. If the concentration of salts in the solution is stronger, there will be a stronger flow of electrons.

A salinity controller monitors and shows the EC level in the solution at all times, and operates injection pumps which add concentrated nutrient solution to the solution in the system when the level falls.

EC will increase if temperature increases. Because of this, it is necessary to provide temperature compensation in the salinity control system. This is usually calculated on the basis of 2% per degree centigrade.

A salinity controller automatically compensates for EC drop bringing it back to a predetermined level, thus maintaining optimum nutrient levels at all times.

Over a period of time, there can be a build-up of unused salts (i.e. parts of the nutrient solution chemicals which are not used). This can create an inappropriate EC reading which will make adjustments to the setting on your salinity controller necessary. Alternatively the solution needs to be replaced with a fresh solution or the system flushed out with water.

Although salinity controllers can maintain nutrient solutions for periods at optimum levels, it is advisable that chemical analysis of the nutrient solution (for nitrogen, potassium, calcium, magnesium, phosphorus and iron) also be carried out from time to time. In large commercial operations, such a chemical analysis should be undertaken at least every two weeks.

pH Controllers

pH (i.e. the level of acidity or alkalinity) is critical to the growth of many plants. Different plants prefer to grow within different limits of pH. Most plants prefer a pH range of 5.5 to 6.5.

A pH controller is a device linked to an electrode in the catchment tank. The electrode measures the pH of the nutrient solution and relays the reading to the controller. The controller can be programmed to inject predetermined amounts of acidic or alkaline solution into the catchment tank if the pH reaches an upper or lower limit. This way, the pH

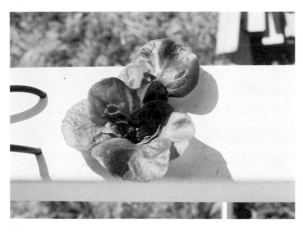

Micro-irrigation tubing feeding nutrient solution into the top end of an NFT channel.

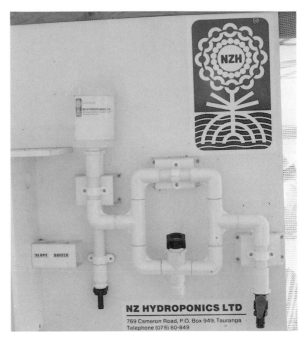

NZ HYDROPONICS LTD
769 Cameron Road, P.O. Box 949, Tauranga
Telephone (075) 80-849

Nutrient supply equipment.

Reservoir underneath the foam box feeds the seedlings via capillary action.

of the solution can be brought back to a level which is suitable for the plants being grown.

If the nitrogen supply in the solution is predominantly potassium or calcium nitrate, the pH will rise during cropping and acid needs to be added periodically to bring the level back to something reasonable. If the pH drops below 5.0, there can be problems with corrosion of parts in the pump.

Usually nitric or phosphoric acid are used to correct high pH in nutrient solutions. They are premixed 1:10 or 1:20 with water and injected into the catchment tank as required, allowing maximum mixing to occur before the adjusted solution is delivered to the plants.

When mixing concentrated acids, always add the acid to the water. It can be very dangerous adding the water to the acid.

Time Clocks

These can range from simple mechanised versions to advanced programmable electronic types that are suitable for multiple operations. They can provide a simple means of automatically controlling such tasks as turning water supplies on and off and adding nutrients. The main problem with such clocks is that they operate on a particular schedule as set by the operator and don't have a monitoring capability that allows them to adjust the timing of their operation according to the plants' requirements.

Computer Controls

Increasingly, commercial and even many amateur hydroponic growers are using computerised systems to undertake tasks such as controlling, monitoring and recording information relating to environmental conditions in the growing area, to the volume and timing of water applications and to the pH and conductivity of both the input and runoff solutions. Specific hydroponic growing computer programs have been developed, particularly over the last few years, that can be used on inexpensive personal computers. A good program can greatly reduce the time and effort expended by the grower in obtaining the optimum growing conditions for his crops.

Specific applications that can be undertaken using computerised systems include:

1. monitoring input solution pH so that when the required pH range, as set by the grower, is breached then a command is sent to a dispenser, such as an injector, to add an acidic or alkaline solution to the input solution to adjust the pH to the desired level.

2. monitoring the conductivity of the input solution, particularly for recirculating systems, to either signal a warning to the grower or to send commands to either a) add more nutrients when EC readings are lower than the desired level or b) flush more water through the system to leach out excess salts when EC readings arc too high.

3. monitoring and controlling, within required levels, environmental factors such as air and root zone temperatures, humidity, light intensity etc. This can be achieved via the computer controlling air vents, heaters, misting systems and other automated equipment.

4. controlling and monitoring the frequency and volume of water application, and monitoring water runoff in run-to-waste systems as a means of determining water use.

5. providing a record of environmental conditions experienced and nutrients used in producing each crop.

Additional information such as crop yields and production times could be added manually to the computer record to provide a complete crop history for future reference.

Current research in Europe and the USA has also indicated the potential of such systems to monitor

Nutrient solution tank.

Prefabricated fibreglass tank and pump.

Prefabricated tanks.

and control the level of individual nutrients, and that this could be extended to adjust required nutrient levels to match differing weather conditions.

Sumps/Storage Tanks

Tanks are frequently too small for the system they are used in. The size of the tank depends on:

* How much water the plant uses (fast growing crops use more)
* How much water is lost through evaporation (depends on temperature in the growing environment)
* Method of applying nutrient solution (capillary feed results in less loss through evaporation)
* Whether you are using a closed or run to waste system
* Type of medium (media such as perlite or rockwool which retain a lot of moisture require less frequent irrigations than media such as coarse sand).

As a general guide:
In aggregate culture— 91 litres (20 gal) per square metre of growing area in cool climates; 136 litres (30 gal) per square metre in warm climates.
Volume should be enough to completely fill the beds one and a third times (i.e. liquid volume plus the volume of solids in the media equals the total volume of the tank plus 33%).
A tank 5450 litres (1200 gals) in size will supply a gravel bed 105 m × 0.6 m × 0.3 m deep (350 ft × 2 ft × 1 ft).

Materials for Tanks

Metal tanks (even galvanised) are not recommended. Chemicals in the nutrient solution make metal tanks more susceptible to corrosion than metal tanks which hold drinking water.

Concrete The major disadvantage of fresh concrete is its lime content, however, weathering before use will eliminate this problem. Here are a few ideas for concrete tanks:

* A large concrete pipe turned on end and concreted in the base is a relatively inexpensive way of making a tank.
* A septic tank, or prefabricated water tank are other alternatives.

Fibreglass or plastic A variety of prefabricated tanks are available, some designed for holding water or chemical sprays, some for other purposes. These are ideal for hydroponic systems but can be relatively expensive.

10   Greenhouse Operation

Greenhouses are used to control the growing environment—therefore they regulate plant growth. They can make the following possible:

- Growing a crop out of season
- Growing a crop faster
- Growing a crop in a locality unsuited to that crop.

Hydroponic culture in a greenhouse has the added advantage that the nutrient solution does not become diluted by rain.

Though greenhouses are normally used to keep plants warmer than the outside environment, they may also be used to regulate other aspects of the environment including:

- Cooling
- Light—controlling intensity and/or day length
- Humidity
- Balance of gases in the air—in particular carbon dioxide
- Exposure to pest or disease organisms.

Greenhouses

A greenhouse is an enclosure made of material transparent/translucent to solar radiation. The covering limits the amount of heat loss due to convective cooling by the wind, as well as reflecting some long wave radiation emitted by the crop and air (depending on cover material). Consequently, when the sun is above the horizon, temperatures build up with heat being transferred to the air, providing significant improvement in the growth of the crop.

A greenhouse responds very rapidly to outside conditions whether changes in solar radiation levels or changing temperatures at night. Without heating, most greenhouses fall to within 1 to 2 degrees C of the outside temperature within 2 hours of sunset.

Greenhouses fall into the following categories:

Glasshouses These have glass walls (at least in part), very effective, long lasting, expensive.

Fibreglass houses Made from fibreglass sheet, cheaper, medium lifespan, poorer insulation.

Coreflute/solar sheet houses These are medium cost, medium lifespan (15 yrs plus), more effective temperature control than PVC or fibreglass.

PVC film (polythene houses) These are made from polythene film, normally over a metal framework (usually a tunnel). Very cheap but lasts only a few years before requiring cover replacement. Insulation is poorer than other coverings.

Other equipment used for environmental control in growing plants:

Hotbeds Heat is provided in the base of a bed (box arrangement) by means of electric heating cables, hot water or steam pipes, or hot air flues. The bed needs to have drainage outlets and be made from a material which will not rot (i.e. brick, concrete, treated timber etc). An ideal size is 1 m × 2 m (3 ft × 6 ft). The hotbed is filled with 8 to 10 cm (3 to 4 inches) of course propagating sand or perlite.

Coldframes A coldframe is almost identical to a hotbed except it is not heated and has a cover/top made from glass, plastic, fibreglass or some similar material. Cold frames might be placed inside or

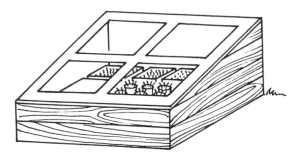

Timber cold frame is a simple, low cost propagating structure for the home gardener to raise plants in.

Fibreglass or PVC sheet

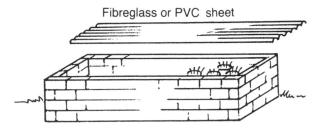

Brick cold frame is a more permanent structure which is used to strike cuttings and raise seeds.

Timber frame solar sheet (coreflute) greenhouse.

outside a greenhouse. A simple cold frame can be built for a very low cost and can be used effectively to strike cuttings or germinate seed (though not as effectively as other structures).

Shadehouses Used for protecting young plants, usually after removal from the propagating area and planting up into the first container. Shadehouses allow for plants to be gradually 'eased' out of their highly protected propagating environment to the harsher outside.

Mist systems These involve a series of mist-producing sprinklers which spray the cuttings/seed at controlled intervals. They serve to prevent drying out *and* to keep the propagating plants cool in the leaf zone.

Fluorescent light boxes Plants of many species propagate well under artificial light. The cool white fluorescent tubes are preferable.

Environmental Controls

Greenhouses are used to control the environment in which plants grow. The environment is extremely complex though, and there are many interactions between the different aspects. The amount of light allowed to the plants might affect the temperature. If you close the vents or doors of a glasshouse, you may stop the temperature from dropping, but at the same time, you may be changing the balance of gases in the air. Every time one factor is altered, a number of other factors are also affected.

Greenhouse management involves giving careful consideration to the full implications of every action you take.

Environmental factors which influence plant growth.

1. Atmospheric temperature—the air.
2. Root zone temperature—in the soil or hydroponic media which the plant roots are growing in.
3. Water temperature—the water used to irrigate the plants.
4. Light conditions—shaded, full light, dark.
5. Atmospheric gas—plants give off oxygen but take in carbon dioxide. Animals do the reverse. Normally they balance each other, but when plants are locked in a closed room or house by themselves, they become starved for carbon dioxide as the oxygen level in the 'room' rises.

Shortwall glass greenhouses.

Polythene film, metal hoop frame, tunnel greenhouse.

6. Air movement—mixes gases, evens out temperature.

7. Atmospheric moisture—humidity.

8. Root zone moisture—water levels in the soil or media.

Pest and Disease Control

Pests and diseases can be more of a problem in a greenhouse than outside.

On the one hand, the greenhouse is contained, which means it can be protected from infection (providing you practise cleanliness). Unfortunately, though, once you do get a pest or disease into a greenhouse, it tends to spread throughout the whole house very quickly (partly because the plants are growing so close together, partly because the warmth and humidity of the greenhouse tend to provide ideal conditions for pest and disease problems).

Fungal problems are in particular of great concern in the greenhouse.

Temperature Control

Temperature can be controlled in a greenhouse in several ways:

1. The sun will warm the greenhouse during the day. This effect varies according to the time of year, time of day and the weather conditions that day. The way the greenhouse is built and the materials used in construction will also influence the house's ability to catch heat from the sun, and hold that heat.

2. Heaters can be used to add to the heat in a house. The heater must have the ability to replace heat at the same rate at which it is being lost to the outside.

3. Vents and doors can be opened to let cool air into the greenhouse, or closed to stop warm air from escaping.

4. Shade cloth can be drawn over the house to stop the warm sun penetrating, and removed to allow the sun to heat the house. (Greenhouse paints—whitewash—can be applied in spring for the same effect. The type of paint used is normally one which will last the summer, but wash off with weathering to allow penetration of warming light in winter.)

5. Coolers (blowers etc.) can be used to lower temperature.

6. Watering or misting systems can be used to lower temperature.

7. Exhaust fans can be used to lower temperature.

8. Water storage under the floor or benches of a glasshouse can act as a buffer to temperature fluctuations.

Heat Loss

An important consideration in temperature control is the heat lost through the walls and roof of the house. Different types of materials (e.g. glass, plastic etc.) have differing levels of ability to retain heat. Heat is normally measured in BTUs (British Thermal Units). The table below provides some insight into the respective qualities of different materials.

Covering material	*Heat loss* (BTU/sq.ft/hr)
Glass (6 mm)	1.13
Double layer glass	0.65
Fibreglass reinforced plastic	1.0
Acrylic sheet (3 mm thick)	1.0
Polythene film	1.15
Polythene film (double layer)	0.70
Polyester film	1.05

From *Greenhouse Operation and Management* by Nelson, Prentice Hall.

Heaters

There are two main types of heating systems:

1. Centralised heating system
Normally a boiler or boilers in one location generating steam or hot water which is piped to one or more greenhouse complexes. This is usually the most expensive to install and may be more expensive to operate. There are side benefits though (e.g. steam which is generated can be used to sterilise soil, pots etc). This type of system is only appropriate in large nurseries or hydroponic setups.

2. Localised heating systems
Uses several individual heaters, normally blowing hot air into the greenhouse. Hot air is often distributed through a plastic tube (or sleeve) 30 to 60 cm in diameter which is hung from the roof and has holes cut at calculated intervals for distribution of warm air.

Localised Heaters

The main types of localised heaters are:

Unit heaters
These consist of three parts:

1. Fuel is burnt in the firebox to provide heat at the bottom of the unit (fuel could be gas, oil or other).

2. Heat rises through a set of thin-walled metal tubes or pipes, which heat up.

3. Behind the heated tubes is a fan which blows cold air through the pipes where it is heated and out the other side into the house.

Convection heaters
These are cheap to purchase and consequently are frequently used by hobbyists and small commercial growers.

They differ from unit heaters in that they do not have a built-in heat exchanger. Fuel of almost any type can be combusted in the firebox (e.g. wood, coal, gas oil etc). Hot fumes then pass out of an exhaust pipe which can be placed between rows of plants, above the heater, or wherever desired. The exhaust pipe should be sufficiently long (or outlets placed far enough away from plants), to ensure dangerously hot air does not come in contact with the plants.

A metal stovepipe or insulated ducting is ideal, however, polythene tubing can be used as well.

A potbelly stove or similar could be used as a convection heater.

Electric heaters
In some parts of Australia electricity is cheap. If you happen to have cheap electricity, an electric heater may be considered. These generally consist of a heating element and a fan which blows air across the heating element and into the glasshouse. This type of heater can cost as little as 2 cents per hour to operate, but in some places as much as 15 cents or more. (Costs calculated for operating a 2000 watt heater which would be sufficient to heat a 3 × 4.5 m house.)

Radiant heaters
Low energy, infrared radiant heaters have become popular in the USA in recent years. Growers report significant savings on fuel costs.

Solar heaters
There are several different types of solar heater which can be used or adapted for use in greenhouse heating. The components of a solar heater are:

1. A collector Different types are possible. They are usually panels heated by direct sunlight. The front is transparent to allow light in, the back is black and insulated to stop energy escaping. Light is converted to heat when it is absorbed by the dark surface.

2. A heat store Water and rocks are two of the most common stores. Water can be passed through the collector and returned to a storage tank of water. Air can pass through the collector and return to the storage tank of rocks.

3. A heat exchanger Pipes or tubes can pass through the heat store and out through the greenhouse and back to complete the cycle. A heat exchange fluid, or perhaps air can flow through these pipes.

A back up heater may be needed in conjunction with a solar system.

Light Control/Shading

Natural light levels in some greenhouses may at some times of the year become too great for some plants. Excessive sunlight can also cause problems by heating the greenhouse too much. The need to provide shading will depend on:

- *Construction materials* Fibreglass for instance does not allow as much light into the greenhouse as glass does.
- *Location* Greenhouses in warmer climates more frequently need shading.
- *Aspect* Greenhouses on a north slope running on an east-west line will catch more sun than houses on a south slope running on a north-south line. (N.B. The opposite applies in the northern hemisphere.)
- *Time of year* Shading becomes more critical in summer than in winter.
- *Type of plants* Some plants need shading more than others.

Shading can be achieved by either using shade cloth or painting the greenhouse roof and walls.

Oil-based, water-diluted paints applied in late spring will reduce light significantly through the summer, but through a process of natural weathering, are gradually washed off the greenhouse over the autumn, resulting in a return to normal light transmission in winter.

The only problem with this method is that the paint might not wash off sufficiently if applied too thickly or if expected rains do not occur over autumn.

Shade cloth is a more reliable, but initially more expensive way of shading. Fabrics can be obtained to give precise degrees of shading to suit the

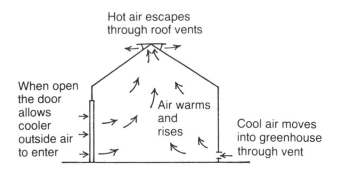

Hot air escapes through roof vents

When open the door allows cooler outside air to enter

Air warms and rises

Cool air moves into greenhouse through vent

Greenhouse ventilation. Adequate ventilation using roof and wall vents and doors is essential to prevent overheating. In commercial systems, ventilation can be automatically controlled.

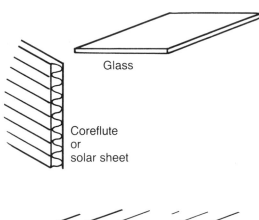

Glass

Coreflute or solar sheet

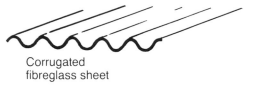

Corrugated fibreglass sheet

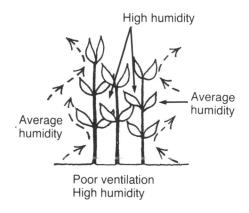

High humidity

Average humidity

Average humidity

Poor ventilation
High humidity

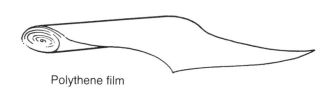

Polythene film

Greenhouse cladding materials. All of these materials are widely used; cost, lifespan, light and heat transmission, and insulation vary considerably.

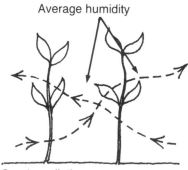

Average humidity

Good ventilation.
Air moves freely between and amongst plants which have plenty of space between them

Ventilation around plants. Plants which are poorly ventilated will be more prone to diseases such as damping off.

situation. The main problem with shade cloth is the difficulty of fixing it to the outside of the house.

Blackout curtains may also be used to control day length.

Humidity

Humidity can be increased in the growing environment in the following ways:

- Using equipment such as humidifiers or fogging machines.
- Periodically spraying a fine mist for a short period through a fine sprinkler head.
- Using a moist mulch around the plants (e.g. woodshavings are sometimes laid on the floor of a greenhouse and kept wet to raise humidity).

Gas Balance

Ventilation supplies fresh air.

The design and use of a ventilation system should be based on the fact that warm air rises above cooler air.

Ideally vents near to the ground are used to let cool air into a greenhouse and vents high on the walls or in the roof are used to expel warm air. The best cooling effect is achieved when low and high vents are both opened to allow the escape of warm air as cool air enters and displaces it from below.

11 Plant Culture in Hydroponics

This chapter deals with some of the specific horticultural techniques used to maximise cropping in hydroponics.

Plant Support

Plants grown in hydroponics tend to be more prone to falling over than plants grown in soil, and thus frequently need some type of trellis support. Water culture methods such as NFT, and light-weight materials such as perlite, vermiculite and rockwool, do not provide firm anchorage of roots in the way that soil does.

- Tall growing plants in particular need support.
- Stronger supports are needed if plants are exposed to wind.
- A greater bulk of plant will need a stronger trellis.

There are two types of trellis systems:

1. Horizontal trellis
Here a mesh of wire, nylon or some other material is supported above the plants in one or two layers (depending on the height of the plants and the amount of support needed).

Carnations, capsicums and other small bushy plants require this type of trellis.

2. Vertical trellis
This may consist of similar mesh material stretched along a row, or alternatively, single wires stretched along a row with support posts at each end.

Vertical trellis can also be hung from the ceiling in a greenhouse.

- Tomatoes may be grown on wires tensioned and spaced at 50 cm intervals. The stems are tied to the wires as they grow.
- Cucumbers require greater support and are either grown on a vertical mesh, or on wires at a 15 to 20 cm spacing. The wires should be tied together every 20 to 30 cm to form a mesh and give additional support.
- In large systems wires need to be connected to turnbuckles so they can be tensioned if they loosen.

Young cucumber on vertical trellis.

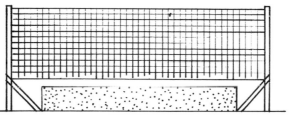

Vertical mesh trellis

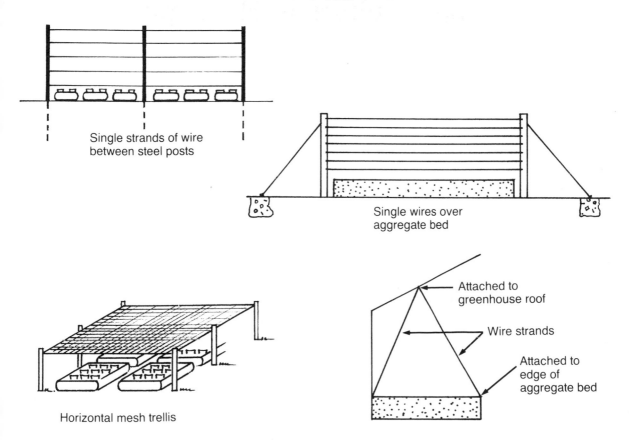

Single strands of wire
between steel posts

Single wires over
aggregate bed

Attached to
greenhouse roof

Wire strands

Attached to
edge of
aggregate bed

Horizontal mesh trellis

Trellising methods using either mesh (wire, nylon etc.) or single strands of wire or twine.

Pruning

Plants are pruned for one of the following reasons:

1. To remove dead or diseased vegetation
This is done so that disease does not spread. Any dead or diseased stems, leaves, fruit or flowers should be cut cleanly from plants and disposed of as soon as it is noticed, irrespective of the crop.

2. To rejuvenate a plant
Young lush growth is always healthier than old tired wood. A rose for instance can have its life extended, and health improved, if old wood is continually removed over a period of years and replaced by younger wood.

3. To control the direction or shape of growth
A plant can be made more bushy by removing the terminal bud of a shoot or stem. When the tip is cut or pinched out, side shoots are forced to develop so that several shoots occur where before there was only one. If you want a taller, less bushy plant,

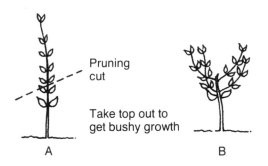

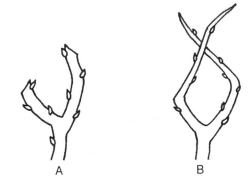

Pruning cut

Take top out to
get bushy growth

A   B

Pruning to encourage compact and bushy growth. Leggy, upright
growth will result in fewer branches, flowers and fruit.

A   B

Pruning to inward pointing buds makes new growth grow
inwards.

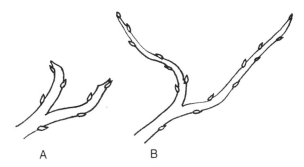

Cut to a bud
and at an angle
to ground

Always prune to a bud to reduce stem dieback. Cuts should
be made at an angle to the ground to prevent stem rot.

A   B

Pruning to outward pointing buds makes new growth grow
outwards.

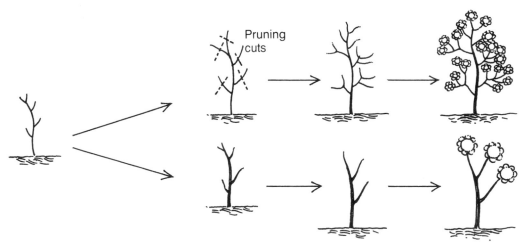

Pruning
cuts

Pruning to influence the size of flowering. Reducing the number of buds and branches will result in fewer, but larger, flowers
and fruit.

side shoots are removed so that there are fewer
growing points (e.g. this is done with tomatoes until
they establish and begin flowering).

4. To control the type of growth
Some plants produce flowers and fruit on growth
which is in its first year (i.e. on year-old wood).

Other plants produce flowers and fruit on growth which is in its second year (i.e. two year-old wood).

By knowing the type of wood on which flowers and/or fruit occur, you can prune a fruit or flower crop to maximise quantity and quality of production.

Raspberries

Raspberries produce fruit on two year-old wood. These should be pruned each winter as follows:

a. Remove wood which produced fruit last season (because this will be 3 years old next season and won't fruit much at all then).

b. Leave the strongest growths of 1 year-old wood (because those will be 2 years old and will produce fruit next season).

c. Leave the strongest half of the new growth which emerged over the past season (i.e. 1 year-old wood), because those growths will produce fruit the season after next.

Chrysanthemums

Chrysanthemums produce flowers on the tips of young growth. The more tips a bush has, the greater the number of flowers it will have, but the smaller each flower will be.

a. If you require a large quantity of flowers, you will remove the terminal bud when you plant a young plant, and periodically pinch out the growing points in the developing stages of the plant. You must cease removing the growing points when flowers start to develop though, or you will be removing flower buds.

b. If you require less flowers, but larger and of better quality, you should cease pinching out terminal buds much earlier.

Pollination

Some plants can have problems with pollination, which result in a reduced number of fruit. Corn, strawberries, tomatoes and cucumbers may be affected in this way, particularly if grown in a greenhouse which has reduced air movement and limited access to pollinating insects. The following methods may be used to help pollination in these and other problem situations:

• Fans to increase air movement.
• Vibrating the flowers by tapping them with a stick or shaking them with your hand (not too hard though or you will damage the plants).
• Releasing bees into the greenhouse.

• Moving pollen physically from plant to plant with cotton wool or some similar material.
• Reducing humidity (which can cause pollen to stick on the plant it comes from and not move to where it is needed).

If you are planning to do any of these things, they must be done at the appropriate time, when the plant is receptive (e.g. tomato pollination should be done late morning, under sunny conditions when the petals of the flowers are curling back).

Carbon Dioxide Enrichment

Plants need carbon dioxide in the same way that humans need oxygen. Without a good supply of carbon dioxide growth will slow.

In some crops and in some localities, yields can be significantly increased by increasing the level of carbon dioxide in the growing environment. This is of course most suited to a sealed greenhouse. In an enclosed environment such as a greenhouse, there is a real danger of plants becoming starved for carbon dioxide. If vents to the outside are closed, the plants will in their normal course of growth gradually deplete carbon dioxide until they reach a level where growth is slowed.

The optimum level for most crops will be around 1000 to 1400 ppm (although natural levels are only around 300 ppm). Nutrition and water demand may increase when carbon dioxide is used.

Methods of supplying carbon dioxide are:

1. At the same time heating a greenhouse: burn a hydrocarbon fuel such as kerosene or propane.
2. Place containers of dry ice in the greenhouse.
3. Release gas from pressurised cylinders.

Carbon dioxide enrichment can benefit the crops below as follows:

• Commercial tomato growers in northern parts of the USA claim crop increases of 20 to 30%.
• Lettuce and cucumber yields increase up to 30% in cool climates.
• Carnations crop faster, have stronger stems and will give production increases of up to 30%.
• Roses under 1000 ppm carbon dioxide levels over winter in cool climates have increased production, improved quality and shorter cropping times.
• Chrysanthemums have stronger and longer stems and crop faster.

Transplanting

Whenever you transplant a seedling into hydroponics there will be some 'shock' effect which is detrimental to the plant and will result in either:

1. Some die back on the root system
—some of the root hairs and perhaps root tips may die, *or*
2. A break in the growth
—growth will slow or cease for a period.

This shock effect will normally be unnoticeable with hardy and easy to grow plant varieties, but can be significant in some situations.

Transplant shock can be minimised by following these rules:

* Don't disturb roots any more than is necessary.
* Use young plants growing in hydroponic media such as Growool where possible, so that the propagating medium can be retained and most of the roots do not have to be exposed.
* Roots should be exposed to the air for the absolute minimum amount of time.
* Don't transplant in hot, windy or dry conditions.
* If planting into NFT, have the system running before you start transplanting.
* If planting into aggregate, apply nutrient solution before transplanting.
* If planting onto rockwool slabs, soak the slabs with nutrient solution before transplanting.
* If you damage or prune the roots of a transplant, cut a corresponding amount of the top back before transplanting.
* Plants which are more susceptible to transplant shock can be sprayed with a mist of water (not nutrient solution!) just before transplanting.
* Irrigate plants immediately after transplanting.

Managing Plant Health

Diagnosis of Problems

Problems fall into three possible categories:

1. Nutritional—Either too little or too much of one or several particular nutrients is available.
2. Environmental—The environmental conditions are not suitable.
3. Pathological—One or more organisms are interfering with the health of the plant (such organisms are called 'pathogens').

It requires a great deal of knowledge and expertise to be able to diagnose plant troubles. Do not expect to develop such ability quickly. The first and perhaps most important skill to develop is an ability to inspect a plant and look for the tell-tale symptoms which can provide an indication of what might be wrong.

The table at the top of the next page provides a systematic approach to inspecting plants which you suspect (or know) might be unhealthy.

You should look at each of the 'items' one at a time, following the guide given by the 'method of inspection' column.

Tell-tale Symptoms

1. Wilting
a. Insufficient water in the soil
b. Leaves drying out faster than the water can be taken up (too hot)
c. Something stopping water going up the stem (e.g. borer, disease etc. in lower part of plant). *Take a closer look!*

2. Yellow leaves
* **If older leaves**
a. Lack of nitrogen (feed with a nitrogen fertiliser)
b. Lack of nitrogen caused by wet soil—wet soil stops nitrogen being taken into the plant (improve drainage or reduce watering)
c. Chemical damage
d. Soil very dry
* **If younger leaves**
a. Iron deficiency
b. Other nutrient deficiency
c. Chemical damage

3. Look to see if the damage is distributed evenly over plant.
—On one side only
—On the top only
—On the most exposed parts
—*Is there a pattern?*

4. Look to see if damage has only just happened . . . or has it happened in the past?
—The appearance of the growing tips tells you the current condition
—Young shoots indicate a healthy plant overcoming past problems
—Excessive side shoots lower down indicate disruption of hormone flow in the plant.

Item	Method of inspection	What to look for
Leaves	View old & young leaves—both above & underneath	Burning; Discolouration; Holes; Leaf drop; Insects—live or dead
Stems	View top to bottom, push foliage out of the way. Binoculars for tall plants	Stem rot; Spots or other markings; Suckering; Side shoots; Thin or thick stems
Growth Habit	Stand back & view, look at where strong growth is & direction of buds	Is it balanced? Appropriateness for type of plant (bushy for shrub, strong terminal growth for tree, etc.); Growth rate
Soil	Feel surface of soil, push finger 2-4 cm below surface. Remove plant from pot	Moisture/dryness; Hardness, root density; Burrows; Wet/dry spots
Roots	View holes at bottom of pot. Remove plant from container. View surface of soil	Root tip burn; Rotting; Distribution of roots—even? Discolouration; Growing tips; Visible presence of insects, nematodes etc.

Plant Health Report Form

The following form can be used to make a systematic study of a problem when it arises. By working through this form, you are forcing yourself to consider everything which should be considered. Unless you are an expert on pest and disease problems, it can be easy to overlook something important if you do not take a systematic approach such as this.

Report by .... Date ....

Location ....

Plant name: Genus .... Species ....

   Common name ....

Condition of plant (tick)
Very healthy ( ) Healthy ( ) Medium health ( )
Sick ( ) Very sick ( ) Almost dead ( )
Dead ( )
Maturity Young ( ) Mature ( ) Old ( )

Estimated height .... Estimated width ....
Estimated lifespan ....

Problem   *Extent of problem*
Existing/Developing/Extensive/Slight
Chewing insects
Dead parts
Sucking insects
Wood rot
Fungal disease
Water stress
Cold
Heat

Recommendation
High priority/Medium priority/Low priority
Remove plant
Spray chemical
Pruning
Change cultural practice

Details of action to be taken: ....

....

Equipment needed ....

Time required ....

N.B. The above form is not comprehensive. Many more alternatives could be listed under problems and recommendations, and perhaps the format could be changed to suit your particular purpose.

Pests

The term plant pests can include a wide range of organisms including:

- Insects which feed on plants or which transmit other problems such as fungal and virus diseases from plant to plant.
- Animals which cause physical damage by digging around plants, knocking plants or eating plants (e.g. goats, birds, dogs etc).
- Animals causing burn to plant tissue by urinating on them (e.g. dogs).
- Man causing physical harm to plants by compacting soil through over-use, knocking and damaging plant tissue, transmitting diseases to the vicinity of 'clean' plants, and through other forms of mismanagement.
- Snails, slugs, nematodes, yabbies, wood lice, mites and other small animals feeding on plants, transmitting diseases etc.

Feeding Habits

The following list may assist in quick identification of insects and other pests causing damage to a plant. They are grouped below according to the type of plant damage which they cause. The list is not exhaustive, but it should cover most common types you will encounter.

Insects (and other pests) which chew above ground
Armyworm, bee, bugs, beetles, caterpillars, crickets, cutworm, earwig, beetle, grasshopper, leafminer, leafroller, leaf skeletoniser, sawfly, slug, snail, springtail, weevil.

Insects (and other pests) which suck plant parts above ground
Aphis, harlequin bug, lace bug, leafhopper, mealy bug, mite, psyllid, scale, squash bug, thrip, tree hopper, whitefly.

Insects (and other pests) which feed below ground
Root aphis, root nematodes, root borer, rootworm, root weevil, woolly aphis, wireworm, beetle larvae.

Borers
Codling moth, bark beetle, corn earworm, white pine weevil, melon worm, longicorn beetle, European apple sawfly etc.

Common Pests and Their Control in Hydroponic Culture

Aphis
Small insects which cluster in large numbers on tender growth (typically on tips of growing shoots, flower buds and occasionally roots).
Can usually be controlled with a safe pyrethrum spray.
Malathion will give good control (but should not be used on food crops close to harvest).

Birds
Birds will attack and eat fruits from many plants including tomatoes and strawberries.
Greenhouse crops are protected by the greenhouse cover.
Bird netting is an effective control but can be expensive.
Regular picking of near ripe fruit will minimise the problem.

Cabbage white butterfly
This is the caterpillar of a white butterfly. See caterpillar (below).

Caterpillars
Chewing grubs which eat foliage and sometimes other plant parts.
Control safely with a spray of Dipel (brand name). (Dipel is a bacteria (*Bacillus thuringiensis*) which attacks and kills caterpillars, but has no effect on any other type of insect or animal.)
Malathion or carbaryl will give good control, but shouldn't be used on food crops close to harvest.

Crickets
Are not a frequent problem, but can occasionally occur in large numbers eating anything in sight. Malathion is an effective control.

Grubs
Grubs are the larvae of insects (many different types) which burrow inside fruits, stems or other plant parts.
As they are on the inside of the plant, most insecticides will not kill them.
Can only be controlled by either removing and burning infected parts, or treating with a systemic insecticide such as rogor (Dimethoate).

Leafhoppers
Tiny insects feeding on the lower surface of leaves causing major mottling or flecks on foliage.
Spray with carbaryl or malathion.

Scale insects appear as small hard shields clinging to the surface of leaves or stems.

Thrips cause flecking on leaves and flowers on a wide range of plants.

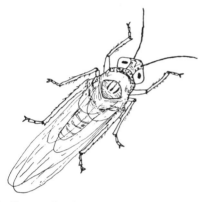

Potato leaf hopper. Leaf hoppers cause mottling on foliage.

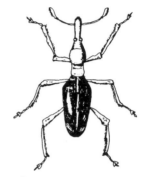

Sweet potato weevil.

Spotted cucumber beetle attacks a wide range of plants. Usually occurs in large swarms in spring and late summer.

The effects of a leaf miner insect, caused by larvae tunnelling through the leaves.

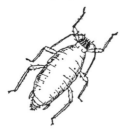

Aphis are small insects usually seen in clusters around shoots and flower buds.

White fly congregate in swarms on tomatoes, beans and other plants. Effects include mottling of leaves and honeydew secretion (which attracts aphis and scale).

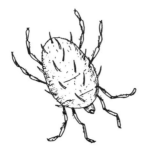

Red spider mite outbreaks mostly occur in hot, moist conditions. Parasitic mites give successful control when released into the greenhouse.

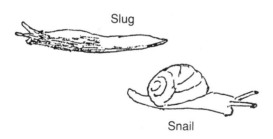

White Butterfly Grub

White Butterfly

Cabbage white butterfly. The caterpillar of this butterfly can cause significant damage to foliage.

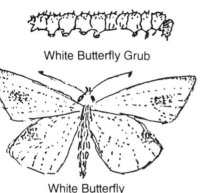

Slug

Snail

Slugs and snails chew holes in leaves and may completely destroy young plants.

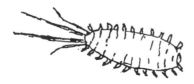

Mealy bugs often occur in the warm, moist conditions of greenhouses.

Tomato damaged by birds.

Leafminers
Insects whose grubs burrow tunnels through the leaves. Tunnels appear white or clear at first.
Spray with diazinon or malathion.

Mealy bug
Small fluffy scale-like insect (with a cotton wool-like covering).
Sucking insect related to scale and aphis.
Occurs in moist organic material (such as wood or peat moss).
Occurs on protected underside of leaves in humid or moist, warm conditions.
Control with malathion.
Regular sprays of pyrethrum will give a safer, though not quite as thorough control.

Mites
These are tiny spiders, virtually impossible to see with the naked eye, though in large numbers they can cause a haze of red colour.
They can attack foliage, fruit and other plant parts on many different crop plants.
They occur in hot, moist conditions.
Control safely by releasing parasitic mites which feed on the plant pests.
Spray with malathion, dimethoate or difocol.

Red spider—see mites.

Scale
Shield-like insects which attach themselves to the surface of stems, fruits and leaves.
Control by smothering with a spray of white oil.

Thrip
Small flying insects which suck plant sap causing flecking on flowers or foliage of many different types of plants.
Spray with pyrethrum, rogor or malathion.

Whitefly
Small white flying insects which move in great numbers when disturbed.
Control with malathion.

Diseases

Plant disease is generally distinguished from insect and other pest problems. Plant pests actually eat the plant, or break the plant by standing on it (as does the human pest). Plant disease is far more subtle, disturbing the microscopic physiological processes which go on within the plant.

When a plant is diseased, it may be affected by one, two, or more different problems. It is often difficult to identify what is wrong with a plant clearly, because the problem is in fact a combination of problems:

A possible scenario is outlined in the example below.

* The plant is weakened by poor nutrition.
* Excessively wet conditions create an environment conducive to the growth of an infectious fungus.
* The plant, weakened by poor nutrition, is infected by the fungal disease which develops in wet conditions.
* The roots begin to rot through fungal attack.
* Because the roots are damaged, the plant does not take in water and nutrients as well as it would normally.
* The leaves of the plant are infected by a second disease because of the above situation which has made the plant weak and less able to repel infection.

Disease organisms will usually fall into one of the following groups:

Viruses are very small microscopic particles composed of nucleic acid and protein. They exhibit many, but not all characteristics of living organisms, and as such, are sometimes called a life form. Viruses can mutate. They cause many serious diseases, frequently causing variegation or mottling of leaf colour. Some viruses are considered beneficial because of the variations they provide in leaf colour. Whether considered beneficial or not, viruses cause a general weakening of plants they infect, making the plant more susceptible to other problems, and frequently stunting growth to some degree.

Bacteria are some of the smallest living things, being just single-celled organisms. They enter plants through stomata or wounds (they cannot break directly through the cell walls of the 'surface' of a plant. Bacteria can cause rots, blights, spots, galls, scabs and other symptoms. (N.B. Fungi can also cause many of these.)

Fungi are chlorophyll-less members of the Thalophyte plants. They are either parasites (living on live tissue), or saprophytes (living on dead tissue). There are over 15 000 species known, and many are responsible for major plant diseases. They are thread-like organisms which grow amongst the tissue from which they derive their nutrition. (The individual threads are known as mycelium.) To reproduce, they grow fruiting bodies from a mass of mycelium, and spores are produced in these fruiting bodies.

Nematodes are microscopic worms which feed in the intercellular spaces, causing breakdown of cell walls. They generally enter plants through the roots, through wounds or stomata (different types of nematodes have different standard methods of entry). Nematodes are much less of a problem in hydroponics than in soil.

Common Terms Used to Describe Diseases

Rot Decomposition or decay of dead tissue.
Spot Well defined grey or brown dead tissue surrounded by purplish margins (or margins of some other dark colour).
Shot hole Dead tissue in a spot cracks and falls, leaving a hole in the leaf.
Blotch Fungal growth appearing on the surface of a dead spot.
Blight Quick death of complete parts of a plant. The disease pathogen develops very quickly. e.g. leaves die and fall.
Wilting Drooping of leaves and/or stems.
Scorch Similar to blight but leaf veins are not affected. Leaf tissue dies between the veins, or along the margins.
Scald Whitening of surface (or near surface) cell layer on fruit or leaves.

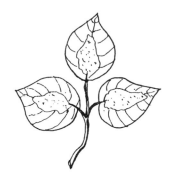

Leaf scorch can be caused by low moisture levels.

Collapse of the plant can be caused by excessive water around the roots.

Wilting can be caused by lower water levels around roots, or wind/heat drying the top of the plant faster than the roots can take up replacement moisture.

Damping off—fungal rot of the base of a young plant caused mainly by one of five different types of fungi.

Blast Unopened buds or flowers die suddenly.

Die back Death of growing tips, moving down through the plant (i.e. the terminal buds die, followed by the death of the stems and lower parts of the plant). Die back can occur to just part of the plant, or in severe cases can continue moving through the plant to the roots.

Damping off Sudden wilting and falling over of young plants, due to tissue being attacked by fungal disease near the soil line.

Mummification Diseased fruit dries up, becoming wrinkled and hardened as it shrinks.

Canker Death of a restricted area of woody tissue— usually a callus of healthy growth forms around the edge of the canker.

Bleeding A substance is exuded from a diseased part of the wood. Only refers to exudation which is not resinous or gummy.

Gummosis Bleeding where the exudation is resinous or gummy. (Gummosis is called resinosis on conifers.)

Firing Leaves suddenly dry, collapse and die.

Rosetting Spaces between leaves on stem do not develop—buds and leaves become squashed together all within a short section of stem.

Mosaic Mottling of yellow and green on leaf surface.

Dwarfing Plants not growing to full size.

Fasciation Round plant parts such as stems become distorted and turn broad and flattened.

Physiological Problems

There are a number of environmental factors which can damage a crop if not properly controlled. Frost or sun may burn fruits or foliage, fruit can crack and leaves can discolour. Some of the more common problems are detailed below:

Cracking

A lack of water or an excess of water can cause the skin of various crops to split. Freshly harvested carrots sometimes split. Tomatoes which are suffering from a lack of water and are exposed to high temperatures may split.

Blossom end rot

A common problem with tomatoes where the bottom of the tomato turns brown or black and leathery in appearance. This occurs typically where there is a low supply of calcium combined with irregular growth, causing stress in the plant.

Frost burn to the tip of a young bean plant.

Blossom end rot on the base of a tomato.

Irregular and variable water supply and variable temperature conditions are also often associated with this problem.

Crooking

This is where fruit becomes distorted (e.g. when cucumbers become excessively curved). Crooking has been attributed to poor control of temperature, moisture or nutrition.

Common Diseases and Their Control in Hydroponics

Alternaria

A blight commonly affecting leaves, sometimes stems. Symptoms are usually spots, often developing concentric rings as they enlarge.

There are many types of alternaria. Most are controlled with Zineb. A copper spray will control some.

Anthracnose

There are two different groups of anthracnose diseases:

1. Symptoms are dead spots
2. Symptoms are improper development of some part of the plant (e.g. a raised border around a depressed central area of undeveloped tissue).

Can be controlled by various fungicides. Some types are controlled by copper sprays, others by Zineb or other chemicals.

Lesions on tomato caused by anthracnose disease.

Lesions on the pod of a bean caused by anthracnose.

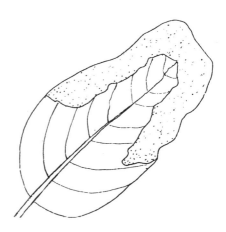

Leaf burning or dying back from the tips and margins can be caused by anthracnose or potassium deficiency.

Botrytis

A grey fluffy mouldy growth occuring on stems, leaves, flowers or fruits.

Occurs in wet, humid conditions.

Affected parts should be removed and burnt immediately.

Can be controlled by Benlate (i.e. benomyl) though this chemical can be very dangerous and its use should be minimised.

Grey mould (botrytis) on lettuce.

Grey mould (botrytis) on strawberry.

Downy mildew

Upper surface of a leaf shows yellowing or dull patches with a greyish mould growing underneath.

Occurs under moist conditions.

Control with Zineb.

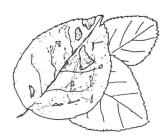

Downy mildew on rose. A problem in moist conditions, appearing as a greyish mould underneath the leaf, and as dull or yellow patches on the surface.

Fusarium

Symptoms can include foliage yellowing, stunted growth, wilt and leaves dropping.

Hygiene will usually control fusarium.

Phytophthora

There are several forms of phytophthora ranging from ones which rot the stem of young seedlings to others which impair the uptake of nutrients in very large plants.

Symptoms are frequently dramatic and can cause sudden death.

Remove infected parts and sterilise infected areas. Fongarid will effectively control some types of phytophthora and slow the spread of others.

Powdery mildew

The main symptom is a white powdery growth on leaf surfaces.

Occurs in warm, moist, humid conditions.

Sulphur sprays or dust will usually give control.

Powdery mildew on apple. A fungus which attacks a wide range of plants. Usually indicated by a powdery grey covering on leaves.

Rhizoctinia

Symptoms are brown or black dead spots or rot, normally on leaves or stems.

Can be controlled with Benlate (benomyl) or terraclor.

Scab

Patches of discoloration develop into spongy, blister-like scabs.

Can affect leaves, stems or underground parts.

Remove and burn infected parts.

Spray with dithane (Maneb).

Smut

Black spots with cracks developing in the spots to reveal a sooty black powder.

Control with Maneb.

Yellowing or paleness between the veins on a leaf indicate iron deficiency when occuring on young, tip foliage, or nitrogen deficiency when occurring on older, lower leaves.

Black spot, a common fungal disease on roses, especially in warm, humid conditions.

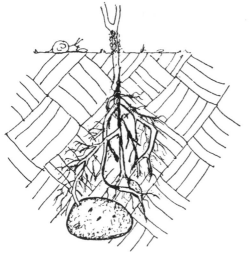

Sclerotinia rot indicated by the black markings on the roots and tuber of a potato.

Verticillium wilt

Symptoms may be as mild as slight paleness in foliage to drooping of leaves, stunted growth, browning between the veins of a leaf and death. Symptoms can be slow or reasonably fast to develop. Infects a wide variety of crop plants.

Infected plants should be removed and burnt.

Infected areas should be sterilised before replanting.

Virus

Symptoms can be any type of abnormal growth such as discoloration of foliage, twisted or stunted growth etc.

Once a plant has a viral disease it is virtually impossible to eliminate it from that plant.

Prevent spread by controlling sucking insects (in particular aphis).

Some plants (e.g. strawberry) deteriorate with the virus over a period of years. Control in such instances involves replacing plants every few years with verified virus-free stock.

Control Techniques

The main ways of controlling pests or diseases are as follows:

1. Sanitation
2. Resistant plant varieties
3. Biological controls
4. Soil drenches/dips
5. Chemical controls.

Rust on chrysanthemum. Orange-brown powdery spots indicate the presence of this fungus which occurs on a wide range of plants. Controlled by sulphur sprays, Mancozeb or Zineb.

Characteristics of Pesticides

Consider the following before deciding on using an agricultural chemical. Your judgment of what to use should balance all of these factors with safety to yourself, your staff, your customers and the environment. The people from whom you buy chemicals should be able to show you documentation on these details.

Toxicity

This is a measure of the pesticide's capacity to poison. This will, of course, vary from one organism to another—it may be very poisonous to one type of insect, but not to another. Toxicity to insects is not always directly related to toxicity to people, domestic animals or wildlife.

Spectrum of activity

This is the range of organisms which it affects. Insecticides such as pyrethrins or dichlorvos are broad spectrum (i.e. they kill a wide range of pests). Chemicals which kill only a small range of insects are called 'narrow spectrum'.

LD50

LD50 is a measure of the toxicity to mammals. It is a measure of milligrams of poison per kilogram of body weight required to kill 50% of test animals. It is generally tested on mice or rats to obtain the LD50 reading. Dermal LD50 is the result obtained by subjecting animals to a dose of the chemical through the skin. Oral LD50 is the result obtained by subjecting the animals to a dose of the chemical through the mouth.

Persistence

Most pesticides will change form gradually after application. The effect of the chemical on organisms it contacts will therefore gradually be reduced. Persistence is a measure of how quickly or slowly the effectiveness of the chemical declines. Persistence is rated in terms of 'half life'. Half life is the length of time from application till the time when the chemical has half the effect it did when it was first applied. Dieldrin for instance has a half life of over 100 years, making it very persistent. Malathion has a half life measured in weeks. Some chemicals have a half life measured in hours.

Volatility

This is how easily the chemical becomes a gas. Volatile poisons are more dangerous to work with (e.g. dichlorvos), because they can readily be inhaled.

Repellency

This is the chemical's ability to repel insects from the place where it is applied. Pyrethrins for instance repel insects such as mosquitos and flies.

Flushing action

This is the tendency of the chemical to excite insects and make them leave places where they are hiding (e.g. making cockroaches leave cracks and crevices).

Knockdown action

This refers to the chemical's ability to quickly incapacitate the insect, i.e. whether it kills quickly or not.

Phytotoxicity

This refers to the harmful effects the chemical might have on plants (e.g. some types of chemicals sprayed under certain conditions will cause burning or other damage to plant foliage, growing tips etc).

Insect Control

The following steps should be followed:

1. Detect the problem
2. Identify the insect involved
3. Find out about the biology of the insect
4. Consider how important it is to control the insect
5. Consider the alternative control methods
6. Select the most appropriate method and carry out what action is necessary
7. Evaluate.

Forms of Applied Insect Control

1. Mechanical Control

This involves using specific physical equipment or techniques such as insect screens, plant enclosures, metal shields (on building foundations), sticky bands in the path of insects etc. The key to mechanical control is to use the appropriate method at the appropriate time. *Timing is very important!*

Some specific examples include:

• Banding the legs of a bench with a sticky layer to prevent and trap insects crawling up onto the bench (e.g. ants).
• Draping young plants with a covering of cheesecloth will discourage cicadas.

Thrip damage on strawberry. (Chapter 11)

Aphis and sooty mould on citrus. Aphis feed off the sap of plants, leaving a sugary secretion known as 'honeydew'. Sooty mould is a fungus which lives off the honeydew. (Chapter 11)

Left: Powdery mildew on zucchini. (Chapter 11)

Below: Young NFT lettuce crop. (Chapter 12)

Cucumber in aggregate provides excellent results. (Chapter 12)

Silverbeet in gravel. NFT and rockwool have also shown good results. (Chapter 12)

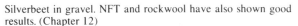

Advanced and newly planted cucumber crops growing in rockwool slabs. (Chapter 12)

Tomato in aggregate. This system provides excellent results, although NFT is the most commonly used commercial method throughout the world. (Chapter 12)

- Wrapping the trunk of a transplanted plant can prevent some types of borer attack.
- Paper or plastic collars around a plant will discourage movement of cutworms.
- Tree-wound paints can provide a barrier to wood borers and some types of ants.

In some situations, irrigating an area heavily will kill off insect populations (perhaps flood irrigating a system if the medium has become heavily infested).

In situations where there are wetlands close to crops, pests may be breeding in those wet conditions—draining a swamp can reduce insect populations which breed there.

Raising or lowering temperatures can also be used to kill insects (e.g. in seed or grain, temperatures over 140 degrees F may kill insects without damaging the seed). Usually low temperatures will slow or stop insect activity, but without killing them as do high temperatures.

Certain types of radiation (e.g. gamma rays or microwaves) may be used to control some types of insects (e.g. gamma rays can make some insects sterile).

2. Cultural Control

Cultural control is a long term approach to managing insect populations. It is based on the concept that the best methods of growing plants will stop insect populations from developing in large numbers.

Cleanliness is an important part of cultural control. This relies on removing infected plants or parts of plants as soon as they are found (e.g. infected fruit should be picked and burnt as soon as it is noticed).

Crop rotation is another inportant cultural practice, even in hydroponics. The basis of crop rotation is to avoid growing consecutive crops in the same place if they share a pest or disease problem. By following a crop of lettuce, for instance, with a crop of tomatoes, the pests which are a problem on lettuce (which may remain on your property after harvest), have nothing to grow on while the tomatoes grow. Hence the lettuce pests die out.

3. Biological Control

This involves manipulating biological factors to control insect populations. This includes:

- Using resistant varieties of plants bred or selected because of their ability to withstand pests.
- Using predators which attack or cause harm to the insects (e.g. Dipel is a commercially available spray of bacteria which attacks and kills caterpillars. Some ladybirds attack and kill some scale.)
- Manipulating the environment (i.e. destroying environments close to your crop where the pest or disease might breed, planting companion plants amongst your crop etc.) with the aim of encouraging or discouraging certain insect species.

4. Legislation

Governments pass laws to restrict the movement of material which tends to carry pests.

Quarantine regulations provide for material to be kept in a separate area for a time and be inspected for pests before being released into the community.

Other regulations can ban the import of certain materials or the entry of unauthorised persons into certain areas.

Summary of Insecticides

The most commonly used insecticides fall into one of the following groups:

1. Inorganic insecticides
e.g. arsenic trioxide, boracic acid
These are generally persistent (they remain as a poison for many years, often hundreds of years). They vary a great deal in their toxicity to mammals. Some are very poisonous, others are not.

2. Botanical insecticides
e.g. natural pyrethrins
Extracted from certain types of daisy plants (genus: Pyrethrum). These chemicals are generally not very toxic to mammals, and are not persistent (i.e. they break down to harmless compounds within a very short period of time).

3. Organochlorine insecticides
e.g. aldrin, chlordane, dieldrin, heptachlor etc.
Mammalian toxicities range from medium to very highly toxic and the persistence is generally very long. These chemicals can remain active for hundreds of years and should not be used.

4. Organophosphate insecticides
e.g. chlorpyriphos, diazinon, dichlorvos, fenitrothion, fenthion, malathion (i.e. maldison), temephos, trichlorphon
Most are short to medium term in their persistence (lasting up to a couple of months). Toxicities range from moderate to very high.

5. Carbamate insecticides
e.g. bendiocarb, carbaryl, methomyl, propoxur etc. Persistence is short to medium term and toxicities are mainly moderate.

6. Synthetic pyrethroids
e.g. permethrin, bioresmethrin, tetramethrin etc. Mammalian toxicities are generally low but persistence in some can be several months (but not years).

Disease Control

Diseases can be controlled in much the same way as insects, either by chemical pesticides, which have obvious drawbacks, or by non-chemical means such as changing environmental conditions or physically restricting the spread of disease.

The following measures are commonly practised to control diseases in hydroponic farms:

- Sterilise the system or greenhouse between crops and hence eradicate disease spores. Wash with an antiseptic solution at least, but beware of fumes.
- Keep tools and equipment clean. Always wash after use. Sterilise tools periodically by washing with an antiseptic solution.
- Make sure shoes and hands are washed clean before entering work areas.
- Be sure that your plants are not diseased (only purchase quality, preferably guaranteed healthy stock).
- Ensure good ventilation around plant leaves and stems.
- Don't get leaves wet. It is better to irrigate with drippers or sub-irrigation. Wet foliage is more susceptible to disease.
- Trim damaged or broken plant parts with a sharp knife or secateurs. Rough or torn tissue is more susceptible to disease attack.
- Remove any diseased or dead plants or plant parts without hesitation. Often you need to be ruthless to save the rest of your crop.

The Lifecycle of a Disease

Whatever method you use to control a disease, it is valuable to understand when and how it infects your crop, and what stages it goes through before and after it is a problem to you.

You may, for instance, be able to attack the disease and kill it before it even infects your crop, or you may be able to stop it reaching your crop if you know where it is coming from.

Stages in Development of a Typical Fungal Disease

1. Inoculation
Occurs when the pathogen comes in contact with the plant. Any part of the pathogen which can attack the plant is called the 'inoculum'.
If the inoculum lays dormant over winter and infects the plant in spring, this is called the primary inoculum, and it causes a primary infection.
Inoculum produced from this infection is called secondary inoculum and can cause secondary infection of the plant.
Inoculum may be present in the soil or in dead plant material near to the plant being affected; or it may be brought in to the area with seed, new plants, soil, on the wheels of a car, on boots or shoes, or even carried by the wind.
Inoculum can survive on weeds or infected plants nearby, and move onto cultivated plants when conditions are favourable.

2. Penetration
Pathogens move into plants by breaking through the plant surface, or by entering through wounds or natural openings (such as stomata).
Some fungi only penetrate through one of these methods.
Bacteria mainly enter through wounds.
Viruses and some microorganisms (microplasmas and some bacteria) enter through wounds made by vectors. (A vector is a disease carrier; e.g. aphis carry viruses, they inject their mouthpiece into the plant creating a wound and placing the virus inside.)
Nematodes normally enter through direct penetration.

3. Infection
This is the process by which the pathogen establishes contact with the cells or tissues which it is going to affect. In this stage the pathogen grows and invades parts of the plant.
Changes to the plant can be either obvious or

obscure at this point. You might see discolouration or necrosis as the disease moves through the plant *or* it may be that the changes are microscopic and necrosis or other symptoms are not seen until the next stage (growth and reproduction).

4. Growth and reproduction

The pathogen now grows and develops within the part of the plant which it inhabits.
It then begins to reproduce itself.

5. Dissemination

Spores or new organisms produced in the growth and reproduction stage are moved to other places where they can sooner or later infect a new plant. Mostly this dissemination is carried out by agents such as wind, water, insects, animals or man.

Water Management

Water Requirements

Plants need both water and oxygen in their environment. The trick to successful plant growing is often to provide the proper delicate balance between these two. Too much air usually means too little water; and too much water usually means too little air.

In aggregate culture, you should usually mix a well-draining medium (e.g. gravel) with a water-retaining medium (e.g. vermiculite) to gain the required balance of water retention.

In many fruits water constitutes 90% of the total weight; for leaves this is 80%, and for seeds 10%.

Apart from its role in the composition of plant parts, water is also important for the movement of nutrients into the plant and of waste products out. Everything in a plant moves in dissolved form. If water is not constantly replaced, the cells lose turgidity and the plant wilts.

Water Excess

Symptoms: Development of leggy seedlings. This usually happens when plants are close together and the soil is warm and moist, as in glasshouses.
Appearance of growth cracks (in tomato fruit, cabbage heads or carrots).
Increasing cell size.
Long internodes (longer gaps between buds on stems).
Bursting cells (if you look under the microscope).

This is usually caused by poor drainage or over-watering. Water excess can lead to stunting, die back of the top of the plant and in extreme situations death. There is a greater likelihood of infection with moulds, rots and other fungal diseases in a wet situation.

Water Deficiency

Symptoms: The first symptom is that the growth rate reduces. Leaves become smaller (though still well coloured).
Stems later become slender, flowers and fruit are smaller.
On some watery fruits (e.g. tomatoes, lemons, peaches etc.) the plant sometimes draws water from half-grown fruit causing the fruit to shrivel. Die back from the leading shoots can occur followed by death in extreme cases.
A lack of water can be due to underwatering; a poor root system; excess drainage or sometimes extreme heat (i.e. water is sometimes evaporated out of the leaves faster than it can be absorbed through the roots in hot or windy conditions).

Feasibility of Irrigation

Before undertaking or designing an irrigation project it is necessary to undertake some sort of feasibility study as to whether it is desirable to commit resources such as capital, labour, time, land etc. to such a project. For large scale projects this may be undertaken by a consulting firm specialising in agricultural engineering. For small scale projects this is often undertaken by the grower himself. Large scale projects may need to consider far-reaching factors such as topographic features, national and international agricultural and financial markets, social change, transport and communications networks, state and federal policies etc. Whereas for small scale projects you often need only to consider such factors as availability of materials and expertise, installation costs and profitability.

Water Relationships

Before designing or using an irrigation system it is necessary to have an understanding of the relationship between root environment, water and plants. The root environment comprises either:

1. Solid material made up of particles of varied sizes and shapes which fit together imperfectly to form a complex system of pores and channels, providing space within the soil for air and water.
2. An enclosed environment saturated with water in either a gaseous or liquid form (or both in the case of NFT).

With a solid medium, when the pore spaces are filled with water the medium is saturated. This may occur after irrigation or rainfall. A medium will only remain saturated if excess water cannot drain freely. The amount of water which a medium can hold at saturation depends on the volume of pore space available. This is known as the saturation capacity.

Moisture in a solid medium can be classified into three types:

1. Gravity water This water can only remain in the medium for a short time before it drains out under gravity.

2. Capillary water This is the main source of water for plant growth, occuring as a thin film on solid particles or as droplets in the pore space. It is held in place by surface tension. (When gravity has removed all the free water a balance is reached where the surface tension binds all the remaining water so that gravity is insufficient to remove it. This condition is known as field capacity.)

3. Hygroscopic water This is a thin film of water held so firmly to the solid particles that plants can't remove it.

Plants utilise water through a process known as transpiration: the plant acts as a pump, drawing water against the forces holding it in the medium, into the plant roots, stems and leaves from where it is lost to the atmosphere via evaporation (an important factor which is influenced by climatic features such as temperature, humidity and wind). If temperatures and evaporation rates are high, then a plant will require more water from the medium than when they are low. Free water is readily utilised by plants, however increasing suction is required to remove the water held by surface tension. When plants reach a stage where they can no longer draw enough water to provide for their needs then they may begin to droop. This is known as the wilting point. If water becomes available at this stage the plant will recover, however if it continues without water it will reach a point where it is beyond recovery. This is known as the permanent wilting point. The difference between permanent wilting point and the soil moisture content is known as the available water. The amount of water held and the amount that is tightly bound will vary from one medium to another.

The table below indicates soil moisture quantities for some different soils expressed as per cent by weight of dry soil. This way of looking at a hydroponic medium is valuable when planning frequency and intensity of irrigations. Though the information might not be readily available for the medium you choose to use, it is worth making the effort to find out these details in the planning stages of a hydroponic venture.

When to Irrigate

The zone between wilting point and field capacity is important in irrigation, with the aim being to keep moisture levels within this zone. It has been found generally that plants take most of their requirements from the upper half of the root zone and as a consequence only about half of the available water is used. Irrigation is therefore generally required when this approximate half of the available water is used up. The amount of water to be applied to a crop is therefore half of the available water in the root zone of the crop when the medium is at field capacity. Irrigation applications are timed according to how quickly the plants use the available moisture and this is generally dependant on climatic conditions and the availability of nutrients. The rate at which water

Soil type	Saturation	Field capacity	Permanent wilt point	Available water
Fine sand	15–20%	3–6%	1–3%	2–3%
Sandy loam	20–40%	6–14%	3–8%	3–6%
Silt loam	30–50%	12–18%	6–10%	6–8%
Clay loam	40–60%	15–30%	7–16%	8–14%
Clay	40–70%	25–45%	12–20%	13–20%

is supplied by irrigation is also important and is governed by medium infiltration rates, or the rate at which water will pass into the medium. If water is supplied at a rate greater than the medium can absorb it then runoff may occur and water may be wasted. The following table gives an indication of infiltration rates for some media.

Soil type	Infiltration rate
Coarse sand	2500 mm/hr
Fine sand	20–100 mm/hr
Peat	1–20 mm/hr

The ideal situation is where application rates are equal to infiltration rates.

All plants need water to grow, and to survive. The amount of water needed however, will vary from plant to plant. The two main factors which affect how much water a plant needs are:

1. The variety of the plant
Some types of plant have the ability to retain water within their tissues for later use. Other plants are unable to do this.

2. The environment in which the plant is growing
If there is plenty of water available around the plant, then it will tend to remain more moist than in exposed, windy, sunny situations.

A plant can suffer from a lack of water, but it can also suffer from an excessive amount of water.

When you water a plant it is important to strike that delicate balance between too little and too much. Overwatering can be just as bad as underwatering.

Measuring Water Available to Plants in a Solid Medium

Calculating field capacity
1. Wet the medium to near saturation.
   Cover to prevent drying from evaporation.
   Let drain for 2 to 3 days.
2. Take a sample of medium and weigh.
3. Place in an oven at 105 degrees C to dry out. Weigh and record this second weight after drying. (Do not heat at a higher temperature as this can destroy organic material and give a false reading.)
4. Calculate field capacity with the following formula:

$$\text{Field Capacity} = \frac{\text{Loss in weight} \times 100}{\text{Final dry weight}}$$

Calculating permanent wilting point
1. Fill a pot with the medium to be tested and plant a vegetable or flower seedling into it.
2. Grow the plant until its roots appear at the bottom of the pot.
3. Stop watering until wilting occurs. When the plant wilts, seal the surface of the pot with a sheet of plastic to prevent further loss of water through evaporation.
4. Now place overnight in a humid enclosure (i.e. either a humid greenhouse or plastic tent). If permanent wilting has not occurred the plant will recover. If the wilting persists in the morning, you have then reached permanent wilting point. Weigh the medium after removing the plant and its roots.
5. Now calculate moisture content by drying the medium at 105 degrees C to find the final dry medium mass.

Available moisture range
Available moisture range = Field capacity minus permanent wilting point.

Estimating Water Requirements

The amount of water required by a plant is affected by a number of factors including the following:

Type of plant
Some plant varieties use more water than others. Some plants have a greater resistance to dry conditions (cacti and succulents are extreme examples).

Rate of growth
If a plant grows rapidly (perhaps because of its variety, or perhaps due to optimum growing conditions in terms of fertility, climate etc.), it will use water at a faster rate.

Climate
In high temperatures soil loses water through evaporation.
In windy conditions both soil and leaves of the plant lose water faster.
Higher levels of natural rainfall reduce the need to irrigate. (Make sure you know not only what the annual rainfall is, but also what the distribution of rainfall is throughout the year.)

Conditions in the root zone
Does the root zone drain freely?
What is the medium's ability to retain water?
Does the medium repel water when dry (increasing surface run off)?

PART 2   DIRECTORY OF CROPS

Information Sources

The cultural information in the following chapters is derived from the following sources:

Grower Magazine
ISOSC Congress
Plant Science by Hartmann, Flocker and Kafranck
Knotts Vegetable Handbook
Hydroponics for Everyone, Sutherland
Beginners Guide to Hydroponics by Sholto Douglas
Advanced Guide to Hydroponics by Sholto Douglas
Hydroponics Correspondence Course Guidelines, Australian Horticultural Correspondence School
Commercial Flower Growing by Salinger
Personal experience: the author and tutors from AHCS
Keith Maxwell, Greg Seymour, Joe Romer, Rick Donnan, and other Australian hydroponics consultants

Note:

Many of the resources referenced in compiling the following chapters conflicted with each other. It has become increasingly clear that a great deal of work needs to be done before a comprehensive and thoroughly reliable reference to plant culture in hydroponics can be produced. Recognised experts often differed in their opinions on what could or could not be grown successfully, and on the most suitable techniques to use. With the possibility of significant variations between one system and another, you should treat the following information as a serious guide, but one which may require adjustment to your own situation, and experimentation before you will achieve optimum results in your system.

12 Vegetable Crops

Artichoke (Globe) *Cynaria scolymus* Asteraceae

Growing conditions
Perennial, needs moist conditions both in air and root environment.
Does not tolerate extreme temperatures, hot dry conditions reduce tenderness of the crop.

Nutrient requirements
Requires higher than average potassium levels.
pH 6.5 to 7.5

Suitable systems
Perlite at 25 cm depth or greater gives good results.

Planting
Propagate from stem cuttings or offshoots containing roots. Seed-grown plants give unreliable crops.
Replant after 5 years.
Space plants at around 1 metre intervals.

Special cultural techniques
Frost protection and summer shading needed.
Normally cut back hard after harvest in late spring or summer.

Problems
Water stress causes bud not to be compact.
Pest problems can include rodents, snails, slugs, leafminers, caterpillars and aphis.
Disease problems can include fusarium, botrytis and virus.

Harvest and Post Harvest
The swollen, immature flower bud is harvested continuously from late autumn to late spring.
Harvest when buds reach the preferred size.
Crops best in 2nd and 3rd years.

Artichoke (Jerusalem) *Helianthus tuberosus* Asteraceae

Growing conditions
Does not tolerate extremely hot conditions (though it can do well in the tropics if shaded).
Requires temperatures between 19 and 27 degrees C.

Nutrient requirements
pH 6.5
Sensitive to higher than normal levels of boron.
Nutrients as for globe artichoke but much higher phosphorus.

Suitable systems
Does very well in aggregate culture (particularly sand).
Not suited to rockwool or water culture.
Perlite at a minimum depth of 25 cm gives good results.

Planting
Plant divisions at 35-40 cm spacings late winter.

Special cultural techniques
Shade in very hot weather.
Pull media up around stems periodically as it grows to ensure tubers are well covered.
Remove flowering shoots.

Problems
Fungal rots, particularly *Sclerotium rolfsii*, are difficult to control once they attack.
Pests are rarely serious.

Harvest and post harvest
Harvest 3 to 4 months after planting when foliage dies down.

A variety of vegetables growing in NFT.

Asparagus *Asparagus officinalis* Liliaceae

Growing conditions
Grows best at temperatures between 15 and 25 degrees C.
Requires deep, well-aerated medium.

Nutrient requirements
Heavy feeder requiring a higher than average EC.
Phosphorus and potassium should be at high levels.
pH 6.0 to 6.8
Has a high boron requirement

Suitable systems
Asparagus needs to be planted deep.
Aggregate culture is best in a bed at least 25 cm deep.
Coarse sand has been successful.
Sutherland recommends perlite for good results.
Media must be well aerated.
Gravel culture is considered suitable.
Maxwell suggests no advantage over soil, therefore limited commercial prospects.

Planting
Propagated by seed or division.

Seedlings take 2–3 years before the first harvest. Lift seedlings during dormant period (winter), trim roots, cut off remains of old leaf stalks and store in moistened peat moss until buds begin to swell (later winter/early spring), then transplant into hydroponic media spacing plants 15 cm apart.

Special cultural techniques
Intercropping in first 2 years while plants are establishing.

Problems
Occasionally aphis, white fly and caterpillars can be a minor problem.
Insect damage is rarely serious.
There are relatively few fungal problems. In some places crops are sprayed with copper fungicides (e.g. Bordeaux or Kocide) to prevent fungal diseases.

Harvest and post harvest
Yield per unit area is relatively low making it less suitable for commercial hydroponics than other vegetable crops.

Aubergine *see* Eggplant

Bean (Common) *Phaseolus vulgaris* Papillionaceae

Growing conditions
Needs plenty of moisture.
Never let it become waterlogged.

Nutrient requirements
Regular supply of nutrient will result in rapid growth and early cropping.
Phosphorus, potassium and sulphur levels high but nitrogen not as high as with other vegetables.
The ratio of nitrogen to potassium should be roughly equal.
Sensitive to excessive boron.
EC should be around 4.0 mS/cm early in the crop, decreasing to 2.0 at harvest.
Yields decrease significantly at high EC levels close to or after flowering.
pH is best around 6.0 and never below 5.5.

Nutrient solution as follows:

Nutrient	ppm	Nutrient	ppm
Nitrogen	180-270	Iron	3
(as nitrate)		Copper	0.05
Phosphorus	40	Molybdenum	0.05
Potassium	210-350	Manganese	0.05
Calcium	140-200	Zinc	0.05
Magnesium	30-45	Boron	0.05

Suitable systems
Beans yield prolific crops under hydroponic systems—at the height of the season, the first beans are ready for picking 8 to 9 weeks after sowing. While all varieties perform well, climbing varieties offer the advantage that they do not take up as much room.
Most aggregate media 10 cm or more deep give excellent results.
NFT, sand, sawdust and most aggregate systems which have been tried have been successful.
Seeds have been germinated in NFT.
Maxwell suggests sand and perlite.
In the Netherlands, yields of climbing beans in rockwool have been better than in soil. Slabs used were 7.5 cm deep and 15-20 cm wide with 4 to 5 plants per slab. Slabs were heated at 15 to 18 degrees C in the early stages.

Planting
Seeds should be sown singly, at a spacing of 10 cm between seeds.
pH levels should be maintained at 6.0; pH below 5.5 will significantly affect growth during early stages.

Special cultural techniques
Trellis is needed, particularly for climbers which can grow up to 2.5 m tall.

Pests
Red spider—minute insects on the underside of leaves, which cause leaf mottling and eventual death. They can be detected by the presence of a reddish tinge or webbing under the leaf. Spray with malathion; alternatively a population of predatory mites could be released into the greenhouse.
Bean fly—larvae of this fly cause damage to the plant by burrowing into the stems. Control by spraying with malathion.
Thrips—These tiny insects reduce pod set by damaging the flowers. Spray with malathion.

Diseases
Mosaic viruses pose a significant problem to bean growers. There are several strains which can infect the plant via aphis transmission. The common mosaic bean virus causes new leaves to crinkle and stiffen; older leaves have chlorotic mottling and underturned margins. There are no satisfactory remedies for viral diseases, however mosaic-resistant varieties have been developed.

Varieties
Different varieties need different temperature conditions.
Flat pod varieties (e.g Kwintus) have been grown successfully in the Netherlands in rockwool.

Beetroot *Beta vulgaris* Chenopodiaceae

Growing conditions
It will grow in semi-shade (making it adapted to intensive culture).
Full sunlight is not necessary, but reasonable light levels are preferred.

Nutrient requirements
Needs a good supply of potassium and calcium.
Will also use chlorine and sodium more than many other plants.
Has a high boron requirement (0.25 ppm or higher).
Responds to high levels of manganese, copper, iron and molybdenum.
pH 6.0 to 6.5.
Will tolerate very high EC levels (over 5.0 mS/cm).

Suitable systems
Can give excellent results in most aggregate culture medium (minimum depth of 10 cm), though not

any better than in soil culture.
Some suggest it takes too much space and too long to grow in hydroponics.

Planting
Sow seeds direct, using twice as much seed as will be needed, into aggregate culture. Seedlings should then be thinned to a spacing of 15 cm × 30 cm between rows.
Germination rates can often be poor.
They can be started in sand and transplanted when 6-8 cm high, though transplants might not grow as well as plants sown direct.

Special cultural techniques
Place extra aggregate around the base as the plants develop.

Problems
Pest and disease problems are minimal.

Harvest and post harvest
Commercial viability is unlikely in hydroponics.
Harvesting of large, tender roots can be done nine to ten weeks after initial sowing.

Broad bean   *Vicia faba*   Papillionaceae
Hydroponic culture doesn't give any better result than soil.

Growing conditions
Hot, dry weather reduces cropping.

Nutrient requirements
Similar to common bean.
Tolerates higher levels of boron than the common bean.
pH 6.0 to 6.5.

Suitable systems
Aggregate culture gives very good results, but not discernably better than soil culture.
Media should be 15 cm or more deep.
Not considered suitable for commercial growing.

Planting
As for common bean.

Special cultural techniques
Trellis required.
Shading may be needed.

Problems
Aphis can damage tip growth (control with pyrethrum near to cropping, control with malathion early in the season).
Excess moisture can cause root rot.

Harvest and post harvest
3 to 4 months after planting.

Broccoli   *Brassica oleraceae*—Botrytis group   Cruciferae
Broccoli is easier to grow in hydroponics than other brassicas.

Growing conditions
Sensitive to poor aeration—hence best in the better-draining media with more frequent than normal applications of nutrient.

Nutrient requirements
Good levels of nitrogen and phosphorus during development.
Iron is also important.
Has a high boron requirement (0.25 ppm is suggested).
Heavy feeders requiring a higher than normal EC (up to 3.5 mS/cm early in the crop and up to 3.0 mS/cm at maturity).
pH 6.0 to 6.8

Suitable systems
Most systems are suitable. Aggregate systems are probably best.
NFT growpots have been used successfully.

Planting
Seeds can be sown direct or in tubes of perlite which can later be sat in NFT channels.
Spacing should be 30 × 30 cm.

Special cultural techniques
Plant support is necessary, and may be critical if there is wind exposure.

Problems
Grubs can be a serious problem in the heads—pest control is essential.

Harvest and post harvest
Broccoli heads should be ready for picking 9 to 11 weeks after planting and will bear for a further two to three months.
The heads should be picked well before there is any sign of flowering and should be cut with 5 cm of stalk attached.

Brussels sprouts   *Brassica oleraceae*—Gemmifera Group   Cruciferae

Growing conditions
Brussels sprouts require cool to cold (i.e. frosty) weather to develop adequate, tightly-formed hearts.

Brussels sprouts.

Need a well-aerated medium and frequent irrigations.

Nutrient requirements
Nitrogen, phosphorus and iron are particularly important.
Have a high boron requirement.
Recommended EC of 3.0 mS/cm while establishing, reducing to 2.5 mS/cm when cropping.
pH 6.5

Suitable systems
Media 10 cm or more deep.
Some consider these plants too large for commercial hydroponic growing.

Planting
Direct sow seeds or plant from tubes in late summer.
Final spacing should be 45 × 45 cm between plants.

Special cultural techniques
Some form of support or trellising is essential.

Problems
Amateur gardeners frequently have difficulty getting a clean crop.

Harvest and post harvest
Brussel sprouts take up to seven months to mature. Hearts should be harvested when they are still small and firm as flavour is lost when they mature and open up.

Cabbage *Brassica oleraceae*—Capitata group Cruciferae

Growing conditions
Aeration should be very high.
Constant moisture is important.
Ideally temperatures above 13 degrees C at all times.

Nutrient requirements
Nitrogen, phosphorus and iron are particularly important.
Has a higher than average boron requirement.
EC at around 3.0 initially dropping to 2.5 later.
pH 6.5 to 7.0

Suitable systems
Excellent results from aggregate culture.
Should suit most aggregate culture.
Minimum aggregate depth of 10 cm.
Has been successfully grown on a bench system, similar to lettuce.
Good results have also been obtained from NFT systems.
Compared with soil, production is not normally high enough to justify commercial hydroponic growing.

Planting
Smaller varieties can be sown at a distance of 30 × 30 cm between plants.
Larger varieties will need to be spaced 45 × 45 cm apart.

Special cultural techniques
Trellising is not required.

Problems
Cabbage white butterfly grubs must be controlled. Other pests can include aphis, flea beetles, maggots and cutworm.
Diseases will be better controlled in hydroponics than in soil, however cabbage can be attacked by several fungi including fusarium, downy mildew and alternaria leaf spot.

Harvest and post harvest
Cabbages can be stored for a month or more after

harvest at 0 to 3 degrees C and low relative humidity.

Varieties
There are varieties available to crop at all times of the year.

Capsicum *Capsicum annuum* var. *annuum*
Solanaceae

Growing conditions
Optimum temperatures for fruit development are 22–23 degrees C by day and 18–19 degrees C at night.

Vegetative growth is best at temperatures between 25 and 30 degrees C.

Strongly-growing plants can withstand high temperatures (i.e. over 30 degrees C), although 35 degrees C and above are harmful.

Humidity levels should be maintained at around 75%. Lower levels of humidity may cause flower abortion while higher levels encourage botrytis problems.

Semi-shade is not only tolerated but desirable in warm areas.

Nutrient requirements
Capsicums require a soil pH of 6.0 to 6.5.

Growth is best if the EC reading can be kept low (but still supplying adequate nutrition).

Capsicums growing successfully in NFT system. Commercial success with NFT systems can be variable.

Initially a ratio of 4 parts nitrogen to 1 part phosphorus to 5 parts potassium will encourage vegetative growth. This can later be changed to a higher potash formula to encourage flower formation, e.g. NPK 5:1:10.

Supply nitrogen as nitrate. Do not use ammonium form.

Calcium, magnesium and boron levels should be higher than normal.

Suitable systems
Aggregate systems with most media, 10 cm deep, give excellent results.

Black poly bags filled with sand and drip irrigated have been very successful.

Perlite/sand mix or straight perlite in foam boxes or beds have also given good results.

Rockwool slabs have given excellent results.

While some people claim success in NFT, this method is generally unsuitable for commercial production.

Planting
Seedlings are planted at 30 to 40 cm spacings.

Special cultural techniques
Early forming flower buds are removed to encourage initial vegetative development. The plant should be at least 40 cm tall before flowers are allowed to develop.

Capsicums require a support system. There are two methods which can be used:

1. Vertical string supports Only 3–4 leaders per plant are allowed to grow up the string; side shoots are suppressed at the first or second leaf stage. If a double planting density is used, only 2 leaders per plant are used.

2. Horizontal nets Nets with a mesh size of 20 cm are used to support the plant. Nets should run every 30 cm with the lowest being 50 cm above the floor. Sideshoots do not have to be suppressed under this method.

Problems
Strong winds can be a serious problem.

Insect pests can include aphis, weevils, maggots, flea beetles, leaf miners and caterpillars.

The most serious diseases are virus problems which are transmitted by aphis (for this reason aphis control is important).

Harvest and post harvest
Fruits are mature when they change from a wrinkly appearance to a glossy, dark green texture. Red fruits take a further 6 weeks to develop.

Carrot   *Daucus carota* var. *sativa*   Apiaceae

Carrots are frequently difficult to grow in hydroponics (because roots don't form as well as in soil) though I have seen occasional success achieved by hobbyists.

Short-rooted varieties are much easier in hydroponics than others.

Growing conditions
Warmth, good drainage and good aeration are essential.

Nutrient requirements
Minimise nitrogen, and maintain good levels of phosphorus and potassium.
If you lower levels of calcium nitrate to minimise nitrogen you will also reduce calcium supply. To compensate you must supply additional calcium in some other way.
pH 6.3
EC should never go above 2.0 mS/cm.

Suitable systems
Aggregate culture is the only worthwhile method. Coarse or heavy media do not succeed.
A medium such as 30% vermiculite and 70% perlite may give the best result.
A deep bed is required.
Sutherland reports excellent results with perlite 15 to 30 cm deep, though other authorities report failure in perlite.
Carrots are not a viable commercial crop in hydroponics.

Planting
Sow direct into vermiculite/perlite bed or sand/vermiculite bed.

Problems
While pest and disease problems are relatively few, aphis and leaf hoppers can occur and several fungal diseases can arise from time to time, particularly in excessively wet conditions.

Harvest and post harvest
Carrots can be lifted at any stage of growth.
In a home garden, thinning to allow some carrots to grow bigger will yield smaller carrots to eat.

Varieties
Short-rooted varieties are more successful than deep-rooting types.

Cauliflower   *Brassica oleraceae*—Botrytis group
Brassicaceae

Growing conditions
Needs good aeration.
Root environment conditions must remain relatively constant—irregular growth rate decreases crop production. The optimum temperature both while developing through to harvest is 15 to 20 degrees C.
Crowding is not a significant problem. Cauliflowers will grow closer in hydroponics than in soil.

Nutrient requirements
EC should be between 1.5 and 2.0 mS/cm.
pH 6.5 to 7.0
Iron, phosphorus and nitrogen are most important.
Has a higher than average boron requirement.

Suitable systems
Aggregate—most media are suitable provided you have a minimum of 10 cm.
Successful results have been reported in gravel, sand, and a sand/perlite mix.
NFT has also given good results.

Planting
Sow seeds direct or from tubes in late summer.
Final spacing should be 45 × 45 cm.

Special cultural techniques
Direct sunlight on the curd can cause yellowing (reducing market quality).
Sometimes leaves are tied together over the curd to improve whiteness.

Problems
Most diseases and pests which affect cabbages also affect cauliflowers.
Diseases include phytophthora, root rot and viruses.

Harvest and post harvest
Harvest before curds overmature.
Trim outer leaves and cool with fan-forced air as soon as possible after picking.

Celery   *Apium graveolens* var. *dulce*   Apiaceae

Growing conditions
Prefers cool or part-shade in warmer months.
Good aeration is essential.
Optimum day temperatures are 16 to 21 degrees C.
Temperatures below 10 degrees C can cause seed stalk development.

Nutrient requirements
A good level of nitrogen is essential.
Taste is improved by adequate supply of chlorine and sodium.
Has a higher than average boron requirement.

Celery in capillary-fed foam tub. Blanching requirements make this crop difficult to grow on a commercial scale in hydroponic systems.

pH 6.5

Suitable systems
Good results in most media in aggregate culture (minimum depth of 10 cm).
NFT culture has also given good results in non-commercial systems.
Rockwool slabs have given excellent results.
Commercial viability of celery in hydroponics is questionable.

Planting
Space 12 cm apart.

Special cultural techniques
Plant densely to create blanching effect while growing.
Wrap stems in paper or black plastic for 1 month before harvest to blanch.

Problems
Subject to many different pests, diseases and other disorders.

Harvest and post harvest
Force cool quickly as soon as possible after harvest. Storage at 0–4 degrees C and 90% humidity extends the shelf life considerably.

Chicory *Cichorium intybus* Asteraceae

Chicory is sometimes commercially grown in hydroponics in any of the following ways:

1. Dormant crowns grown in the ground are planted in hydroponics and sprouted—the large head of leaves which emerges is harvested before it bursts open and eaten as a salad vegetable.
2. Seedlings are grown from the beginning in hydroponics to produce crowns which are eaten as a salad vegetable.
3. Seedlings are grown in hydroponics to produce roots which are cooked and eaten like carrots.

Growing conditions
Sprouting crowns: keep at 13 to 15.5 degrees C and in total darkness until the shoots are approximately 18 cm tall, then harvest.

Nutrient requirements
Similar nutrient formulae to lettuce.
pH 5.5 to 6.0

Suitable systems
NFT or semi-NFT (i.e. NFT with the gullies filled with gravel.
Aggregate: must be well aerated and constantly moist.

Planting
Sow seeds in trays or boxes of 60% sand and 40% vermiculite.
Transplant to permanent position later in soil or gravel bed. Grow on to maturity.
If grown in soil, lift crowns and trim off any side shoots.
Store at temperatures between 0 and –5 degrees C for several weeks.
This cold temperature stimulates the development of flower buds.
Wash then transplant into hydroponic media. Maintain a higher temperature in the root zone than in the air above. i.e. 15 to 20 degrees C in the root zone and 12 to 17 degrees C in the air. The primary flower bud develops quickly, swelling to 6 to 8 cm and weighing up to 120 g in 3 to

4 weeks, at which time it is harvested.

Harvest and post harvest
Harvested shoots which are thoroughly blanched have the best flavour.
Flavour deteriorates as the harvested shoots turn green.

Corn (Sweet)   *Zea mays* var. *rugosa*   Poaceae

Growing conditions
Warmth and good light conditions are most important.
Shelter from strong wind is important.

Nutrient requirements
Heavy feeding is required during establishment.
pH 6.0
An EC of 2.5 mS/cm or higher can reduce yield.

Suitable systems
Aggregate—most media should succeed at a minimum depth of 15 cm.
Success has been reported in sand beds.
NFT systems have also given good results.
Yields are relatively low per cubic metre and commercial application in hydroponics is questionable.

Planting
Sow direct into aggregate or into rockwool propagating blocks.

Special cultural techniques
Support (trellis) is required.
Closely planted corn has pollination problems and needs to be shaken to ensure good pollination and a reasonable crop.

Problems
Corn is prone to attack by a range of insect pests, fungi, bacterial and virus diseases.

Harvest and post harvest
Harvest when kernels reach full size and turn yellow. This is best determined by examining directly.
Flavour deteriorates rapidly after harvest. For best flavour eat within 2 hours of harvesting, or freeze on harvest.

Cucumber   *Cucumis sativus*   Cucurbitaceae

Growing conditions
Needs day temperatures of 24–30 degrees C.
Tolerates over 38 degrees C.
Requires high levels of water (i.e. needs frequent irrigations and prefers high humidity).

Semi-shade may be necessary in warm climates or mid-summer.

Nutrient requirements
pH should be around 5.5.
In general, a standard nutrient solution with a ratio of approximately 4 nitrogen to 6 potassium to 1 phosphorus, will give good results.
Ratios between nutrients should be maintained approximately as follows during all stages of the crop:
2 parts K to 1 part Ca
10 parts K to 1 part Mg
The only variation might be a slight increase in the proportion of potassium during fruit formation and development.
While maintaining these ratios you should vary the amount of nutrient powder you dissolve in solution at different stages of the crop to achieve EC readings as follows:
Early while the plants are establishing: 2.0 mS/cm
From when the plants reach about 1 metre tall until 3 to 4 weeks after the first harvest: 2.5 mS/cm
Between 3 and 7 weeks after the first harvest: 2.0 mS/cm
Beyond 7 weeks after the first harvest: 1.7 mS/cm
An EC of 3.0 mS/cm has been found to reduce crop yield.
Keep sodium and chlorine levels as low as possible.
Over 50 ppm sodium can cause problems.
Sulphur is best kept between 30 and 60 ppm.
Nitrogen should be as nitrate and not ammonium.
Iron is needed at higher levels (up to 3 ppm) early in the growing season, but can be reduced as the plants mature.

Suitable systems
Aggregate culture is successful in most media at 10 to 15 cm depth.
Perlite has been successful in commercial production.
NFT systems have also given excellent results but are not as successful as aggregate culture commercially because roots can clog the gullies and impair flow of nutrient solution.
Rockwool has been used commercially in the Netherlands and the UK.

Planting
Seed can be started in rockwool or sand and transplanted.
Direct seeding is effective because seeds are so large.

Blueberries packaged in punnet—packaging is an important aspect of marketing! (Chapter 13)

Strawberry in aggregate pot, sitting in an NFT channel. (Chapter 13)

Amaryllis has been successfully grown in sand and sand/perlite systems. (Chapter 14)

Dutch iris are best grown in drier media such as sand or gravel. (Chapter 14)

Space plants 15 cm apart.

Special cultural techniques
Pinch out terminal buds to encourage branching and stimulate female flower development. (Note: male and female flowers are separate but on the same plant.)

Applications of silver nitrate and gibberellic acid will promote male flowers. Ethephon will promote female flowers.

Trellising is required, but be careful tying stems as they can be brittle.

Problems
Wind protection may be necessary.

Diseases include powdery mildew and downy mildew, anthracnose, fusarium wilt, scab, alternaria leaf spot, bacterial wilt and several virus diseases. Pests include cucumber beetle, squash bug, leaf miner, leaf hoppers, aphis and spider mites.

Harvest and post harvest
Once in production, a crop is picked every 1 to 3 days.

Quality in terms of colour and seed size deteriorates if fruits are allowed to get too large.

Cool and store between 7 and 10 degrees C on harvest (colder temperatures can damage fruit).

Varieties
New mildew resistant strains are easier to grow. More compact-growing types such as apple cucumbers are more adaptable to hydroponics, though other types have been grown commercially with success.

Endive *Cichorium endiva* Asteraceae

Growing conditions
Well suited to hydroponic culture.
Similar growing conditions to chicory.

Nutrient requirements
As for chicory.
pH around 5.5

Suitable systems
NFT pipe systems have given good results.
Aggregate culture has also been successful.

Planting
Similar to lettuce.

Special cultural techniques
Blanched by tying leaves up to stop light reaching the centre or 'heart' of the plant.
Blanching reduces bitterness of the crop.

Harvest and post harvest
Cut at ground level and remove outer green leaves at harvest.

Eggplant *Solanum melongena* Solanaceae

Growing conditions
Needs warmth and low humidity.
Roots require good aeration and drainage but constant moisture and nutrient supply in the root evironment.

Nutrient requirements
Basic nutrient should be similar to that used for tomatoes.

Nitrate deficiency decreases yield.

Nitrate excess also decreases yield and causes high nitrate levels in the fruits.

Cut nutrient solution concentration by around 30% as soon as fruits are seen to be forming. Return to normal feeding after harvest. (You may well have several harvests in a season.)

Optimum nitrate levels are 6–8 mg/litre, under greenhouse conditions in southern France.

EC should be around 2.0 mS/cm.

pH 6.0

Suitable systems
Growing on rockwool slabs has given a significantly increased production over soil cultivation (i.e. 10 cm deep slabs and 2 plants per 90 cm slab). Maxwell suggests rockwool, NFT and aggregate culture as being commercially viable.

Planting
Space 15–20 cm apart normally.

Special cultural techniques
Pinch out side shoots on developing plants (as you do with tomatoes).

This reduces number of fruits, but increases the size of each fruit.

Problems
Verticillium wilt (a common eggplant problem in soil) is very little trouble in rockwool.

Blossom end rot (similar to tomatoes) can be a problem.

Several other insect and fungal problems can occur, though these are not generally as likely as on tomatoes.

Harvest and post harvest
Test maturity by gently squeezing fruit. A slight dent will indicate fruit is ripe.
Cut from plant, do not pull.

The best fruits are dense, rich in colour and firm.
Store at 7 to 10 degrees C and 85% humidity.
Fruit will be damaged by lower temperatures.

Varieties
Numerous varieties are available varying in shape,
size and colour.

Garlic   *Allium sativum*   Amaryllidaceae

Growing conditions
This is a cool season crop, but planted in late autumn
or early spring.
Cooler temperatures are needed to achieve a fast
growth rate.
Higher summer temperatures are needed to initiate
bulb or clove formation.

Nutrient requirements
Similar to onions.
pH 6.0

Suitable systems
Most types of aggregate are successful with a
minimum 10 cm depth.
Maxwell suggests sand culture.
Sutherland reports good results in rockwool slabs,
though this may be questionable for commercial
use due to danger of rockwool fibres adhering to
cloves when harvested.

Planting
Divide and plant cloves in spring.

Problems
Aphis can attack foliage.
Fungal rots can attack roots and cloves in over-
wet conditions.

Harvest and post harvest
Lift autumn-planted crops in early autumn and
spring-planted crops in late autumn. (N.B. It can
take up to 10 months from planting to harvest.)
Store in dry, dark place after harvest.

Leek   *Allium ampeloprasum*   Amaryllidaceae

Growing conditions
Similar to onions, but a cool season crop, planted
in summer for winter maturity.

Nutrient requirements
Heavy feeders needing frequent applications of
nutrient solution.
Phosphorus is most important, nitrogen next in
importance and phosphorus next.
pH 6.5 to 7.0

Suitable systems
Aggregate gives excellent results in most media 10
cm or deeper.
Perlite gives good results.
Good results have been reported on rockwool slabs.

Planting
Sow seed into perlite or rockwool propagation
blocks.

Special cultural techniques
Cutting the tap root will reduce chances of plants
going to seed in warm conditions.
Blanched by placing a collar, or tying paper around
the stem.

Problems
Similar to onions.

Harvest and post harvest
Six to seven months from planting to harvest.

Lettuce   *Lactuca sativa*   Asteraceae

Growing conditions
Growth needs to be fast and at an even rate (will
mature in 40–85 days depending on variety).
Shading may be needed in hot conditions.
The root zone should never overheat.
Most varieties prefer temperatures between 12 and
20 degrees C.
Temperatures over 27 degrees C can affect quality
and cause flower stalk development.

Nutrient requirements
Requires a moderate, standard solution at a uniform
rate (too strong or too weak can lead to irregular
growth).
NPK early in the season 9:1:16.
As growth progresses reduce nitrogen slowly to
reach 15% lower nitrogen at harvest.
Tolerates high levels of boron, but only has a
moderate requirement.
Molybdenum, copper and manganese are more
important than most other minor nutrients.
pH 6.0 to 7.0
Yield has been reduced by EC levels of 2.0 or higher.
Lettuce responds to more frequent irrigations with
a lower concentration nutrient solution.

Suitable systems
Vertical columns have been used in Poland.
NFT has been used in England, Japan and Australia.
Modified NFT with gravel in gullies is very
successful.
Coarse aggregate culture gives excellent results in

Lettuce and other vegetables growing in NFT.

any medium 10 cm deep.
Rockwool gives excellent results and has been used commercially.
Media with a greater cation exchange capacity are not suitable.

Planting
Germinate seed in vermiculite, perlite or rockwool propagation blocks, then transplant into system at 6 to 8 leaf stage.
Sow direct into aggregate beds then thin out.

Harvested NFT lettuce.

Tray of lettuce seedlings in groplugs ready for planting.

Mature NFT lettuce crop.

Special cultural techniques
Remove marked or damaged outer leaves.

Problems
Irregular burst of growth can cause decreased quality or quantity of produce.
Rapidly-grown lettuces are relatively free of disease.
Excess water or poor aeration commonly causes yellow or rotting of the lower (outer) leaves.
Some will burn on leaf tips if exposed to too much sunlight.
Pests include aphis, flea beetles, crickets, spring tails, leaf hoppers, caterpillars, whitefly, slugs and snails.
Aphis is of particular concern because it transmits viral diseases.
Other disease problems include damping off (pythium), sclerotinia, downy mildew, powdery mildew, botrytis, rhizoctinia and anthracnose.

Harvest and post harvest
Are ready to pick after four weeks in summer.
Rockwool grown plants can be harvested with roots intact, still in the rockwool—this significantly improves the keeping quality.
Damaged or marked leaves should be removed on harvest.
Store between 2 and 4 degrees C under high humidity.

Varieties
Hydroponics is especially suited to the production of the small, fancy leaf type lettuces.
Mignonette can be grown all year (with the aid of a greenhouse in cooler climates).
Some varieties are slower bolting, reacting more slowly to high temperatures. These are most suited to grow in warmer months.

Marrow

Vegetable marrow, squash etc. *see* zucchini (treat similarly).
Spaghetti marrow is not as good as other types (according to Sutherland).

Melon *Cucumis melo* Cucurbitaceae

Growing conditions
Hot, dry air environment with frequent irrigations.
Root zone should never dry out.
In hot weather, each plant can use as much as 4 litres of water per day.
In cool temperature climates, substrate warming (to 25 degrees C) is used to start greenhouse crops early in the season.

Nutrient requirements
EC should be kept around 2.0 to 2.5 mS/cm early in the season, then 2.5 or slightly higher once plants have established. An EC of 3.0 or higher can reduce crop yield.
Nutrient solution should be applied at a rate to allow about 20% of each irrigation to run off and be lost. This helps wash away any build-up of sodium, which can be a problem.
Potassium should be increased a little during fruit development.
Nutrition requirements are similar to cucumbers.
pH 5.5 to 6.0

Suitable systems
Rockwool slab culture tends to produce a larger number of smaller fruit than soil culture (for this reason, larger-fruiting varieties are preferred in rockwool). Melons are grown commercially in rockwool in the Netherlands.
Good results in aggregate culture, most media at 10 cm deep.

Planting
Spacing depends on variety.
Seed direct into perlite or rockwool or transplant seedlings.

Special cultural techniques
A plastic collar or mulch between the media and the foliage will help keep air humidity down.
Keep fruit from sitting on moist surfaces.
Trellis must be used to control direction of growth.

Problems
Pests can include aphis, cutworms, leafhoppers and spider mites.
Diseases can include powdery and downy mildew, fusarium and anthracnose.
May need hand pollinating.

Harvest and post harvest
Rock melons are picked when the fruit comes away from the stem easily. They are at their best three days later, after storage at 21 degrees C.
Watermelons are ripe when the surface of the fruit becomes slightly bumpy and underneath becomes slightly yellow.

Varieties
Honeydew melon *Cucumis melo*—Inodorus group
Rock melon, cantaloupe or musk melon *Cucumis melo*—Reticulatus group

Okra *Abelmoschus esculentus* Malvaceae

Growing conditions
Need good aeration and drainage.
Requires frequent irrigations.
Needs ample warmth (around 24 to 26 degrees C).

Nutrient requirements
Good nitrogen supply important.
Okra is a heavy feeder.
pH 6.5

Suitable systems
NFT used in Australia.

Planting
Soak seeds in water for 2 days before sowing.

Special cultural techniques
Requires support system.

Problems
Verticillium wilt is a particularly serious problem.
Several other fungal disease can occur, including fusarium wilt and some leaf spot fungi.
Aphis and a number of other insect pests may present a problem.

Harvest and post harvest
Harvest daily starting 8 to 10 weeks after planting.
If pods are allowed to stay on the plant after they attain full size (i.e. 10 to 15 cm long) quality deteriorates fast.
On harvest, rapid cool and store at 7 to 10 degrees C and 90% humidity. Lower temperature can injure fruits.

Onion *Allium cepa* Amaryllidaceae

Growing conditions
A relatively dry situation—low humidity, good drainage and aeration and minimum irrigations.
Requires good air movement around foliage to minimise fungal problems.

Nutrient requirements
High levels of potassium and nitrogen.
pH 6.0 to 7.0
Manganese, copper, zinc and molybdenum are important micronutrients.
Tolerates high levels of boron but only has moderate boron requirement.
Nitrogen: phosphorus: potassium ratio of 15:3:16.
Reduce nitrogen and potassium levels as the crop develops. By mid-season nitrogen levels should decrease by 20%, and by the end of the season by 30%. Potassium can be dropped by up to 20%

over the total life of the crop.
EC should never go above 1.8 mS/cm.

Suitable systems
Aggregate culture gives excellent results, though not significantly different from soil culture.
Most media should be around 10 cm deep.
Bulb onions take too long in hydroponics, given the crop's value.
Spring onions are quicker and may be viable in perlite, sand or modified NFT (with gravel in gullies).

Planting
Seed can be germinated in aggregate culture, or pre-germinated seedlings transplanted into the system.

Special cultural techniques
Cease irrigations on bulb-forming onions when bulb has attained full size.
Allow the tops to almost completely die down, then lift and store.

Problems
Too much water causes fungal problems.
Pests include aphis, thrip, maggots and cutworms.
Diseases include downy mildew, fusarium, botrytis, smut and several other virus and fungal problems.

Harvest and post harvest
Lift bulb onions after tops die down completely.
Pull spring onions before tops begin to die down.

Pak-choi *Brassica rapa*—Pekinensis group Cruciferae

Growing conditions
Requires a lot of moisture, but reasonable drainage also.
Growth ceases at temperatures below 10 degrees C.

Nutrient requirements
EC 1.5 to 2.0 mS/cm
pH 7.0
Otherwise similar nutrition to cabbage.

Suitable systems
Rockwool slabs have proven successful.
NFT or modified NFT with gravel could be worth trying.

Planting
Can suffer transplant shock.
It is preferable to allow it to germinate in its permanent position.

Problems
As for cabbage.

Harvest and post harvest
Harvest 70 to 80 days after planting.

Parsley   *Petroselinum crispum*   Apiaceae

Growing conditions
Tolerant of cold temperatures.
Good aeration but constant moisture in the root zone.

Nutrient requirements
Similar to carrots.
pH 5.5 to 6.0

Suitable systems
Excellent results by Sutherland in perlite 25 cm deep.
Excellent results in 30% perlite/70% coarse sand at 20 cm depth.
NFT has been used in Australian but root rots are sometimes a problem.
NFT, rockwool and most aggregate systems have been suggested by various hydroponics experts.

Planting
Space at 10 to 20 cm intervals.

Problems
Few pest and disease problems.
Some insects can mark foliage occasionally.

Harvest and post harvest
Cut 70 to 80 days from planting.
Plants can be repicked several times over a season, then replanted for the next year.
Store at 0 to 4 degrees C and high humidity.

Parsley in gravel/perlite medium.

Parsnip   *Pastinaca sativa*   Umbelliferae

Growing conditions
Requires a very deep medium.
Generally unsuited to hydroponics, though some have had success in aggregate culture.
Tolerates cold and frosts.

Nutrient requirements
Phosphorus is needed for good root development.
Calcium, nitrogen and potassium are needed in larger than normal proportions.
pH 6.0

Suitable systems
Commercial viability is highly questionable.
Sutherland reports excellent results in perlite 25 cm deep.

Planting
Sow seed in perlite.

Pea   *Pisum sativum*   Papillionaceae

Growing conditions
Requires good aeration, low humidity and frequent irrigations with nutrient solution under warm conditions.

Nutrient requirements
Calcium, iron and phosphorus particularly important.
Adequate manganese is essential to achieve maximum cropping.
pH 6.0 to 7.0
We suggest trying an NPK ratio of 8:1:5.

Suitable systems
Aggregate culture should succeed with most media at a 10 cm depth, or rockwool.
Not generally suited to NFT (though we have had snow peas reported to have grown well in NFT).

Planting
Sow seed direct into permanent position, or start in rockwool propagating blocks.

Special cultural techniques
Tall types require trellis/supports.

Problems
Relatively few apart from some insects.

Harvest and post harvest
Yield is not high enough to make peas commercially viable in hydroponics.

Varieties
Tall and short varieties are available.

Potato *Solanum tuberosum* Solanaceae

Growing conditions
Tubers must not be exposed to light.
Media should not become too warm, though foliage can withstand heat.
Media must be deep (30 cm or deeper).
Good drainage and aeration are essential.
Some claim potatoes need a shorter growing period in hydroponics compared with soil.

Nutrient requirements
Heavy nutrient requirement.
Requires higher levels of phosphorus, otherwise similar nutrition to tomatoes.
pH must be 5.0 to 6.0.
EC ideally between 2.0 and 2.5 mS/cm.
NPK 7:1:9 (N.B. higher phosphorus than other vegetables).
Heavy feeders, but because they are sensitive to high EC levels, frequent applications of nutrient solution in a very well-drained system will give the best results.

Suitable systems
Aggregate culture or granulated rockwool only are suitable.
NFT or rockwool slabs are unsuitable.
Potatoes grow easily in 50% sand and 50% perlite.
Not suited to commercial hydroponic production.

Planting
Plant sprouting pieces of tuber direct.

Special cultural techniques
Media must be continually pulled up to cover any exposed tubers.

Problems
Prolonged absence of copper in nutrient reduces reproduction of aphis.
Increased zinc in solution also reduces aphis.

Harvest and post harvest
Harvest when tops begin to die down.
Red-skinned varieties have a better keeping quality.

Pumpkin *Cucurbita pepo* var. *pepo* Cucurbitaceae

Growing conditions
Similar to cucumber, but a slightly lower temperature requirement.

Nutrient requirements
pH of 5.5 to 7.5
Nutrition similar to cucumber.

Trellising of pumpkins.

Suitable systems
Rockwool very successful.
NFT channels can become clogged with the large root system, reducing flow of solution.

Planting
Sow seed direct in perlite, rockwool or sand; or transplant seedlings.
Spacing depends on variety.

Special cultural techniques
Trellis is generally required.

Problems
Similar to cucumbers.

Harvest and post harvest
Harvest when fruit stem begins to shrivel by cutting.
Store at 0 to 10 degrees C.

Varieties
There is considerable variation in growth habit from more compact bushes to very large sprawling plants.

Radish *Raphanus sativus* Cruciferae

Some growers have found radishes difficult in hydroponics but very easy in soil. Some have been successful with aggregate culture.

Growing conditions
Shade is needed in hot areas.
Aeration is important.
The texture of the medium is critical to root formation.
Growth must be steady (i.e. at an even pace).

Nutrient requirements
Nitrogen and phosphorus are important.
Iron is often difficult to absorb due to lack of fine root hairs. Iron is important.
Sensitive to low levels of manganese.
Higher than average boron requirement.
pH 6.0 to 7.0

Suitable systems
Most aggregate media 10 cm deep, perhaps best in perlite, gravel or sand.
Not suited to rockwool or NFT.

Planting
Sow seed direct.

Problems
Excess warmth can cause bolting.
Pests and disease similar to turnip.

Harvest and post harvest
Usually 4 to 6 weeks from sowing seed.

Rhubarb *Rheum rhabarbarum* Polygonaceae

Growing conditions
Temperatures below 25 degrees C.
The root environment should be well aerated but with a constant supply of water and nutrient.

Nutrient requirements
Nutrition must be maintained at reasonable levels at all times.
Phosphorus is particularly important.
pH 5.5 to 6.0

Suitable systems
Aggregate culture gives excellent results with most media at 15 cm depth.
Rockwool slabs have been used successfully.
If in NFT, channels must be very wide.

Planting
Plant so the crowns barely appear above the surface of the medium.
Propagated by division.

Rhubarb is best suited to aggregate and rockwool systems.

Special cultural techniques
Shading is sometimes used to get crops in warmer weather.

Problems
Frost and a few fungal rot diseases are the only major problems.

Harvest and post harvest
When leaves turn down on the leaf stem they should be removed by pulling gently from the plant (do not cut).
Stems are eaten but the leaf is poisonous.

Silver Beet As for spinach.

Spinach *Spinacia oleraceae* Chenopodiaceae

Growing conditions
Prefers cool, shaded conditions.
Best between 15 and 19 degrees C.

Nutrient requirements
Nitrogen is most important.

NPK ratio should be 10:4:12.
Sensitive to a lack of manganese, copper, molybedenum and iron.
pH 6.0 to 7.0

Suitable systems
Most aggregate media at 10 cm deep give excellent results.
NFT using Growpots or Vinidex channel.
Rockwool slabs have given excellent results.

Planting
Sow seed in sand or perlite and transplant into hydroponic system at 6-8 leaf stage.
Space plants 8-10 cm apart.

Problems
Chewing insects, slugs and snails can be a problem.

Harvest and post harvest
Normally rapid growing, harvest can begin after 6 weeks and can be continuous.

Sweet potato   *Ipomoea batatas*   Convolvulaceae

Growing conditions
Must have warm dry air conditions and shade in very hot conditions.

Nutrient requirements
Average rate of nutrient uptake—neither heavy nor light.
Potassium, phosphorus, calcium and magnesium are needed in higher than normal ratios.
pH 5.5 to 6.0
EC of around 2.0 mS/cm (sensitive to levels over 2.5 mS/cm).

Sweet potato crop. Good results have been obtained by using sand or gravel culture.

Suitable systems
Sand culture is well suited according to Sholto Douglas.
Has been successful in perlite.
Sand or gravel in foam boxes fed with dripper have been successful.

Planting
Cuttings approximately 20 cm long are half inserted in media and strike easily (cuttings should be shaded until roots form).

Special cultural techniques
Trellising needed.

Problems
Several insect problems including moth grubs, beetles and weevils.
Fungal diseases which cause rot.

Harvest and post harvest
3 to 6 months after planting.

Taro   *Colocasia esculenta*   Araceae

Growing conditions
Grows most rapidly during the tropical monsoon season under wet, hot conditions.
Drainage and aeration must be good.

Nutrient requirements
Requires an acid root zone.

Suitable systems
Run to waste (i.e. open) aggregate systems with sand or gravel have proven best.
Sand or gravel are perhaps most suitable.

Planting
Plant young suckers taken from the base of established plants, or sections of tuber containing a piece of leaf stalk.
Space 30 cm apart and up to 1 m between rows.

Special cultural techniques
Push media up around base of plants as they grow, keeping tubers well covered.

Problems
Few.

Harvest and post harvest
Harvest 6-8 months after planting.
You should harvest around 8 kg per plant.

Varieties
The Dasheen varieties must always remain wet.
The Eddoes varieties tolerate extremes of dry and wet in the media.

Tomatoes growing in rockwool.

Tomato in aggregate culture.

Tomato *Lycopersicon esculentum* Solanaceae

Growing conditions
Requires 21 to 24 degrees C for optimum growth. Growth slows significantly below 18 or above 27 degrees C.
Requires good aeration and drainage.
In very hot conditions, some shading is needed.
Avoid very high humidity.

Nutrient requirements
Regular feeding is needed to avoid stunted growth and reduced cropping.
pH 6.0 to 6.5
Before planting, irrigate the media with nutrient solution to achieve an EC of 5.0 mS/cm. Maintain this feed strength for about a month and then decrease it gradually to 3.0 mS/cm over the next 8 weeks, then to between 2.0 and 2.5 mS/cm over the summer.
The ratio of potassium to calcium should stay at 3:2 throughout the life of the crop (N.B. some sources suggest a K:Ca ratio of 2:1).
Calcium to magnesium ratio should be 4:1.
Potassium to nitrogen ratio shold be 1.4:1 early in the crop but increased to 1.8 to 1 providing higher potassium later in the crop.
Phosphate should be relatively low, at about 40 ppm throughout the crop.
Sodium and chlorine levels should be kept as low as posible.
Trace elements are normally supplied in the following amounts, irrespective of the stage of growth:

Iron	1.0 ppm
Manganese	0.50 ppm
Zinc	0.40 ppm
Boron	0.30 ppm
Molybdenum	0.05 ppm
Copper	0.05 ppm

Some sources recommend iron at levels of up to 5 ppm.
Zinc levels are critical (below 0.25 ppm can cause deficiency and above 1 ppm can cause toxicity).

Suitable systems
NFT—size of fruits decreases towards the bottom end of a channel (hence total production is decreased).
Multi-level NFT has shown great potential for increased production (in Poland).
NFT is the most commonly used method throughout the world.

Aggregate culture—Sutherland reports excellent results in most aggregate culture at 15 cm depth.
Perlite has also been successful.
Rockwool is used commercially in the Netherlands.

Planting
Germinate seed in rockwool propagating blocks or perlite and transplant into your system.

Special cultural techniques
Prune out side shoots until flowering commences.
Trellising is necessary.
Bees may need to be introduced for pollination.

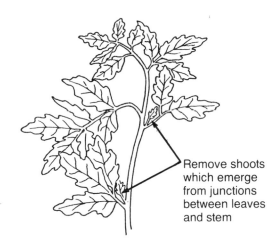

Remove shoots which emerge from junctions between leaves and stem

How to prune tomatoes. Lateral growth should be discouraged until flowering commences.

Problems
Heating solution in NFT led to blossom end rot appearing.
Blossom end rot is encouraged by any stress on the plant.
An irregular rate of growth will enourage blossom end rot.
Birds will attack ripe fruits.
Pollination can be a problem in a greenhouse (wind and insects normally contribute towards pollination).
Don't smoke near tomatoes. A virus carried in tobacco can infect the plants.
Other pests include aphis, fruit fly, potato beetle, corn earworm, leafminer, white fly and mites.
Other diseases include anthracnose, bacterial canker, bacterial spot, blight, fusarium wilt, verticillium wilt and leaf mould.

Harvest and post harvest
Can be harvested green or firm and pink.
Firm ripe tomatoes should be stored at 7 to 10 degrees C and 85 to 90% relative humidity.

Turnip   *Brassica rapa*—Rapifera group
Cruciferae

Growing conditions
Cool conditions are essential for proper development.
Media must be well drained and have good aeration.
Avoid heavy gritty media.

Nutrient requirements
Phosphorus, potassium and iron are most important.
Iron uptake can be a problem sometimes.
Higher than average boron requirements.
pH 6.0 to 6.5

Suitable systems
Perlite or vermiculite (or a mixture) are likely to give the best results.

Planting
Sow seed direct into perlite or vermiculite.

Problems
There are few problems in the edible root, though leaves are often attacked by insects.

Harvest and post harvest
2 to 3 months from planting to harvest.
Cut leaves and wash roots at harvest.

Watermelon   *Citrullus lanatus*   Cucurbitaceae

Growing conditions
As for pumpkin, but higher temperatures.
Ideally temperatures between 21 and 30 degrees C.

Nutrient requirements
pH 5.8
As for pumpkin.

Suitable systems
As for pumpkin.
Vigorous root sytems can block pipes and beds.
Not considered commercially viable in hydroponics.

Planting
Seed direct into rockwool propagating blocks, perlite or vermiculite.

Problems
As for zucchini.

Harvest and post harvest
Harvest when skin starts to become bumpy, and undersurface starts to turn yellow.

Varieties
Smaller bush-type varieties are most suited to hydroponics.

Zucchini   *Cucurbita pepo*   Cucurbitaceae

Growing conditions
Requires a large area per plant to be productive. Good aeration and a constant supply of moisture and nutrient are essential.

Nutrient requirements
pH 6.0
Similar to pumpkin or cucumber.
Nitrogen : phosphorus : potassium ratio should be 10:3:10.

Suitable systems
NFT has given good results, although some growers prefer using aggregate culture because of disease problems.
If grown too long in an NFT system, channels can clog with roots.
Foam boxes filled with aggregate media 10 cm deep have been successful as a run-to-waste system.

Bag culture could be economically viable.

Planting
Seed can be planted direct into aggregate or rockwool.
Space plants at 35–45 cm intervals.

Special cultural techniques
Remove diseased fruits or leaves as soon as they appear.

Problems
Pests include aphis, mites, leafhopper and other insects.
Diseases include powdery and downy mildew, fusarium wilt, gummy stem blight, black rot, alternaria leaf spot, anthracnose and bacterial wilt.

Harvest and post harvest
Fruit needs to be regularly harvested to keep the plant producing well.
Harvest before 20 cm long.

Varieties
Also called 'summer squash'.

13   Berry and Other Fruit Crops

Banana   *Musa acuminata*   Musaceae

Growing conditions
Average temperatures are best between 27 and 29 degrees C.
Minimum temperature of 15 degrees C and maximum of 35 degrees C.
Frost kills the plant.
Temperatures below 10 to 15 degrees C reduce fruit quality.
Humidity should be high.
Root zone should always be moist.

Nutrient requirements
NPK ratio of 12:1:16 is recommended.
pH 5.5 to 6.5

Suitable systems
Due to the size of the plants, hydroponic growing is generally only relevant under glass in cooler climates where bananas would not normally grow.
Not generally considered a commercially viable hydroponic crop.
Perlite at 40 cm deep gives good results.
Scoria at 40 cm deep also gives good results.
Hydroponic bananas have been successful in Iceland.

Planting
Propagate vegetatively by removing suckers which grow from the rhizome beside old plants.
Only take suckers free of nematodes and bunchy top virus.

Problems
Fusarium wilt used to be a problem until wilt-resistant varieties were developed.
Bunchy top virus is a major problem.
Wind protection is essential.

Harvest and post harvest
Fruit takes around 3 months to mature from flowering.
First harvest is within a year of planting.

Banana growing in aggregate under glasshouse conditions.

Varieties
Grow fusarium-resistant varieties such as Giant Cavendish, Valery and Robusta.

Black Currant   *Ribes nigrum*   Saxifragaceae

Growing conditions
Black currants are deciduous shrubs which require winter chilling to initiate fruiting.
In Australia, commercial production has therefore centered on Tasmania.

Nutrient requirements
A recommended NPK ratio of 10:1:6.
pH of 6.0

Suitable systems
Aggregate culture is recommended.
Though little information on hydroponic culture is available, being shallow rooted they should adapt well, though commercial application is doubtful.

Planting
Bushes should be planted between 1.5–1.8 m × 1.2–1.5 m apart.
Either one or two-year old bushes can be planted. One-year old bushes should be 45 cm high and have a minimum of two branches; two-year old bushes should have 4–5 branches, each over 60 cm long.
Immediately after planting, branches should be pruned back to 1–2 buds above medium.

Special cultural techniques
Black currants produce fruit on the previous season's growth. Pruning should therefore encourage a supply of new growth each season. In the second season of growth, weak shoots and some of the older canes should be removed to allow room for new growth. A framework of 6–8 strongly-growing upright canes should be left. In subsequent years, this procedure should be repeated; no basal canes should be allowed to grow for longer than 3 years.

Problems
There are few pest and disease problems.
Poor temperature conditions are the most common cause of crop failure.

Harvest and post harvest
Fruit will mature by early to mid-December in Australia and will be borne on the bushes for a four-week period. The berries should be left on the bush until 99% of the crop is ripe.
Mature bushes should produce up to 3 kg of fruit.

Varieties
Varieties which perform well in Australia are White Bud, Boskeep Giant, Carters Black Champion, Dunnet's and Black Naples.

Blueberry   *Vaccinium* sp.   Ericaceae

Growing conditions
Roots must remain moist at all times.

Nutrient requirements
Blueberries require an acid pH level around 4.0 to 5.0.

Suitable systems
Has been grown with moderate success in 50% sand to 50% peat mix.
Commercial viability in hydroponics is doubtful.

Planting
Bushes should be planted at spacings of 1.5 × 1.5 m.

Special cultural techniques
Pruning of the bush in the first 3 years should be limited to removal of dead and diseased wood. During this period, only the vegetative buds should be allowed to grow (rub off the plumper fruiting buds). After year 3, the bush will have attained sufficient size to permit shaping. In June or July, older wood should be cut back to 30–40 cm to stimulate new shoots. Some branches may need to be fully removed to prevent overcrowding.

Problems
Blueberries are relatively free of pest and disease problems.
One possible problem is the occurrence of botrytis (grey mould), which can affect flowers and ripe berries in wet and humid conditions. Spray with captan.
Birds can be a problem.

Harvest and post harvest
Berries are ready for harvest in mid to late December with the fruit being borne on the bush for a period of 6 weeks.
Berries should be allowed to ripen on the bush.

Brambleberries   *Rubus occidentalis*   Rosaceae
(boysenberry, loganberry, youngberry etc.)

Growing conditions
Root zone must be well aerated but always moist.
A cold period of dormancy is needed.

Nutrient requirements
A NPK ratio of 10:1:10 is suggested.

Suitable systems
Gravel, sand, perlite or rockwool should be successful.
Not suitable for NFT—vigorous root growth would block the channels.
Commercial viability may be limited in hydroponics.

Planting
Plant in rows 1 to 2 metres apart (depending on variety).

Special cultural techniques
Trellis support and wind protection is necessary. Prune annually in winter while dormant, retaining half of the 1st year canes and half of the 2nd season canes. The 2-year-old canes will produce fruit the following summer and should then be removed the next winter to make way for new fruiting wood.

Problems
Some types need bees for cross pollination.

Harvest and post harvest
Pick continuously as berries ripen. Each plant should yield 1.5 to 2 kg per year.

Paw paw   *Carica papaya*   Caricaceae

Growing conditions
Ideal temperatures between 21 and 27 degrees C.
Requires full sun and no frost.
Good aeration and drainage are important.

Nutrient requirements
pH should be around 6.5.
NPK recommended at 7:1:18.

Suitable systems
Sholto Douglas reports excellent results in greenhouse.
Aggregate culture would be the system most likely to succeed.

Planting
Normally propagated by seed.
Plants can be any one of three sex types:
1. Male only
2. Female only
3. Bearing flowers with both male and female parts.
The male flower plants do not bear fruit at all. These plants are discarded as soon as the sex is determined.
Each plant requires a minimum of 3 square m.

Special cultural techniques
Trellis and wind protection are essential.

Problems
Plants become too tall to be managed within a few years.
They then must be removed and replaced.
Mites can be a serious problem—normally controlled with sulphur sprays.
Fruit flies can be a significant pest.
Fungal and viral diseases can also be a problem.

Harvest and post harvest
Trees can bear fruit within the first year and crop continuously, provided growing conditions are maintained.

Pepino   *Solanum muricatum*   Solanaceae

A small bush to 1 metre tall and 1 metre diameter, related to the tomato and producing a small oval fruit similar in taste to some melons.

Growing conditions
Similar root environment to tomato.
A little more cold hardy than tomato.
Can be killed by frost.
Will grow in semi-shade.

Nutrient requirements
As for tomato.

Suitable systems
As for tomato.
Has been grown successfully in gravel and sand culture.

Pepinos have grown successfully in gravel and sand culture systems.

May have some commercial potential, though not seriously tested as yet in hydroponics.

Planting
Plant at 0.5 to 0.8 metre intervals.
Grows readily from cuttings or natural layers.

Special cultural techniques
Trellis is essential.
Stems must be tied up or they will sprout roots wherever they come in contact with moist media. This self-layering leads to a reduction in fruit production.

Problems
Avoid severe cold or heat.
White fly and various other pests and diseases of tomatoes can occur.

Harvest and post harvest
Harvest when fruit turns yellow.
Fruit has good keeping quality under cool temperatures.
Cold temperatures can damage fruit.

Pineapple   *Ananas comosus*   Bromeliaceae

Growing conditions
Day temperatures are best not exceeding 31 degrees C.
Once fruits begin to mature night temperatures should not drop below 21 degrees C.
Dry air environment; moist, well-drained, well-aerated root environment.
It will survive with reduced watering but fruit production decreases.

Nutrient requirements
pH 5.5 to 6.0
High levels of nitrogen and potassium are important early in the crop.
Iron and zinc are particularly important minor nutrients.

Suitable systems
Sholto Douglas reports good results.
Aggregate culture is most likely to succeed.

Planting
Plant crowns (i.e. leafy top cut from fruit) direct in sand/perlite, perlite or vermiculite/perlite, in a permanent position.
Space 50 cm apart.

Special cultural techniques
After harvest, side shoots or suckers develop which produce a second crop about a year later. This second crop is not as good as the first.

Remove and replant after the second crop.

Problems
Mealy bug can cause difficulty.
Several fungal problems may arise including rots caused by Phytophthora species.

Harvest and post harvest
The first harvest is up to 2 years after planting.

Raspberry (Red)   *Rubus idaeus*   Rosaceae
As for brambleberries.

Red currant   *Ribes sativum*   Saxifragaceae
As for black currant.

Strawberry   *Fragaria* sp.   Rosaceae

Growing conditions
Requires good drainage and aeration.
Needs reasonable ventilation (air movement) around foliage and fruit.
A good quality water supply (with a low level of dissolved salts) is critical.
In summer, plantings require approx. 20 litres of water per square metre growing in sand culture.
Ideal temperature for good vegetative growth is 15 to 18 degrees C.
Low temperatures over winter are required to break a dormancy which develops in autumn.
Higher temperatures are required for good crop development.

Nutrient requirements
Strawberries require a pH of 6.0 (a high pH will cause iron deficiency).
Sulphur, boron and mangesium are important minor nutrients.
Lack of boron can result in poor pollination.
Potassium or magnesium deficiencies can cause leaf burn.
Potassium deficiency can cause insipid and soft fruit.
Minimise levels of chlorine.
Phosphorus level should be higher than in the average nutrient mix.

Suitable systems
Commercial strawberry hydroponic systems are based on a trough system.
Troughs, filled with gravel, perlite or granulated rockwool, are typical 10–15 cm × 15–20 cm, with four or five troughs mounted vertically.

Pruning of strawberry runners. Runners should not be allowed to develop, as they deplete the plant's energy resources which are needed for quality fruit development.

Planting

Runners are taken off parent plants mid to late summer and stored between 0 and -2 degrees C until ready for planting.

Only use material which you are sure is free of virus.

New varieties are propagated in tissue culture.

Plant new plants in early autumn. Trim roots to around 8 cm when planting.

Runners which have been established in pots may also be used as planting material. Any flowers on the runners are removed at planting time to prevent premature fruit formation.

Early plantings (late autumn) can give up to double the crop in their first season compared with late plantings (late winter).

Plants are spaced at 35–40 cm intervals.

Special cultural techniques

Remove runners which develop on plants as they will detract from the quantity and quality of the crop (i.e. only retain the main plant).

Cut old leaves off at the end of each season's harvest (late autumn) leaving only emerging new foliage.

Replant every 3 to 4 years (after that time, virus disease is highly likely to be affecting production, even if plants still look healthy).

Some types of media will stick to fruit (e.g. perlite or vermiculite). Laying a plastic mulch on the surface of such media will keep the fruit clean.

Problems

Virus transmitted by aphis is a major problem.

Snails, slugs, birds and various grubs will attack fruit at times.

Fungal diseases such as botrytis can also affect fruit occasionally, particularly under humid conditions.

Harvest and post harvest

Harvest fruit as it changes to red on a daily basis. Pick with stalk still attached.

Pick when colour has changed 60 to 70% pink while some of the fruit is still white and place immediately in a cool place (perhaps 10 to 15 degrees C).

Strawberries harvested at this stage and stored at 2 degrees C will keep for up to 10 days.

Flavour is best on berries harvested when fully red, but storage period is greatly reduced.

14　Flower Crops

Alstroemeria　(Peruvian Lily)　Alstroemeriaceae

Growing conditions
Requires good drainage and constant moisture.
Four weeks or more at 5 degrees C or lower is required over winter to initiate flower buds.
As day length increases, flowering starts and continues while temperatures remain below 18 degrees C.
Often grown in greenhouses.

Nutrient requirements
Suggested NPK ratio 15:1:9.
Only apply nitrogen in nitrate form.

Suitable systems
Not known in hydroponic culture, though it is considered to have potential as a commercial hydroponic crop.

Alstroemeria is a potential hydroponic crop, suited to perlite or sand culture.

Recommended for sand or perlite culture in beds, foam boxes or plastic bags.

Planting
Propagated by division of rhizomes.

Special cultural techniques
Grow through a horizontal trellis.

Problems
Relatively free of pests and disease.
White fly, caterpillars and aphis can occur under warm conditions.
Regular applications of fungicide and insecticide are used when grown commercially under glass.

Harvest and post harvest
Harvest by pulling off stems (this stimulates further flowering).
Harvest when first flowers are opening and strip lower leaves from stem before placing in water in a cool position.

Amaryllis (Hippeastrum)　Amaryllidaceae

Amaryllis is grown commercially both as a cut flower and for bulb production.

Growing conditions
Minimum root temperature of 20 degrees C.
High humidity is preferable.
Root zone must have constant moisture but be reasonably well aerated.
Night air temperature should not drop below 18 degrees C.
Carbon dioxide enrichment has been used in some greenhouses in Europe to maximise growth.

Nutrient requirements
Nutrient requirement is low in early stages but should be increased as the crop develops.

Suitable systems
Aggregate culture is probably most appropriate.
Sand and sand/perlite have been used successfully.

Planting
Propagate from offsets or scale cuttings.
Plant out in beds mid to late winter. Spacing will relate to the size of the bulbs being planted.

Special cultural techniques
Ventilation can be important, but shading is only ever used in extreme situations.
Horizontal mesh trellis is important, among other reasons, to control fungal diseases by improving air movement around the plant.

Problems
Pests include mites, thrip and aphis.
Several fungal diseases including fusarium, as well as virus, can occur.

Harvest and post harvest
Lift bulbs late autumn and dry quickly at 23 degrees C before marketing or storing for replanting.
Harvest flowers when buds become loose, but before they open.
Store at 7 to 10 degrees C.

Anigozanthos   Haemodoraceae

Kangaroo paw has great potential as a cut flower. Perhaps the greatest limiting factor is 'ink spot' fungal disease, which is difficult to control in most soil plantings. Hydroponic culture may offer a way of overcoming this disease.

Growing conditions
Needs a well-drained and aerated root zone.
Requires low humidity.
Optimum day temperatures are between 18 and 27 degrees C.
Requires a sunny position.
There is considerable variation in specific climatic preferences between varieties.

Nutrient requirements
Unknown in detail.
Iron is important, phosphorus should not be too high.

Suitable systems
Gravel, sand or rockwool are suggested.

Planting
Propagate by division or tissue culture. Seedlings are variable.
Spacing would depend on variety.

Problems
Main problem is ink spot fungal disease which is very difficult to control.

Harvest and post harvest
Harvest continuously over warm months when first flowers open on a stem.

Varieties
A range of hybrid varieties under the name 'Bush Gems' is relatively resistant to ink spot.

Antirrhinum (Snapdragon)   Scrophulariaceae

Growing conditions
Cool greenhouse crop, a perennial usually treated as an annual, providing cut flowers mainly winter and spring.
For winter flowering varieties temperatures in the range of 10 (night) to 16 (day) degrees C are best. For spring varieties 16-22 degrees C and for summer types 18-24 degrees C.
For the first 4-6 weeks of growth all types respond well to a night temperature of 16 degrees C.

Nutrient requirements
Requires high calcium.
pH 6.5
Sensitivie to high EC levels.

Suitable systems
Gravel and sand culture have been very successful.
Modified NFT (with coarse sand in the channels) should succeed.
Rockwool should succeed.

Planting
Sow seed in a container of sand, or peat and sand and transplant when small (approximately one month after sowing) with a ball of medium around the roots to their permanent position, with a spacing around 20 × 20 cm.

Special cultural techniques
Pinch growing tip out at 6-8 cm tall to cause branching.

Problems
Seed is very fine so sub-irrigation is best for watering at this stage.

Harvest and post harvest
Flowers are cut when the bottom florets are completely expanded, while the tip florets are in tight bud.
The cut stems should be put immediately into water and ideally stored at an air temperature of 4 degrees C.

Aster   Asteraceae

Growing conditions
An annual producing flowers in summer and autumn.
Some shade in hot weather is beneficial.
Night temperatures above 23 degrees C result in weaker stems and smaller flower heads.
Constant rate of growth is important to achieve good crops.
Avoid rapid temperature changes.

Nutrient requirements
Heavy feeders.
Require high levels of calcium.
pH 6.0 to 6.5

Suitable systems
Few references available specific to hydroponic growing.
We suggest rockwool and gravel culture would be appropriate.

Planting
Grown from seed then transplanted when small either bare rooted or with ball of germination medium around roots.
Spacing depends on variety, but generally around 20 × 20 cm.
Optimum germination temperature is 21 degrees C.

Special cultural techniques
Each shoot from the main stem is disbudded to a single flower.
Remove any suckers which develop.
Grow through one or two layers of horizontal trellis (15 cm mesh).
Artificial lighting to extend day length and stimulate flowering is sometimes used.

Problems
Pests include, slugs, snails, aphis.
Diseases include anthracnose, botrytis, fusarium and verticillium wilt, powdery and downy mildew, and viral diseases.
A regular spray program is necessary, particularly to control aphis and botrytis. Be careful to follow spray recommendations as aster foliage is susceptible to chemical spray burn.

Harvest and post harvest
Cut when outside petals are fully open but some inside petals are still folded and retain a slight tinge of green.
Strip leaves from bottom one third of stem, bunch and stand in water, ideally in a cool room at 5 to 8 degrees C.

Begonia

Growing conditions
Does not tolerate intense light conditions.
Requires shading in warm or mild climates.
Air temperature is best between 21 and 27 degrees C.
The root environment should be more moist than average, but well drained. (At lower temperatures, root environment needs to be drier.)
While some types will survive at low temperatures, all are frost tender.

Nutrient requirements
Has low iron, high potassium requirements.

Suitable systems
Capillary-fed aggregate systems are excellent.
Has been grown very successfully in perlite and 50/50 perlite and sand.

Planting
Propagate by seed, leaf or stem cuttings.

Problems
Pests include aphis, scale, mealy bug etc.
Diseases include botrytis, anthracnose, various root rot fungi, verticillium wilt, powdery mildew, bacterial spot and crown gall.

Harvest and post harvest
Several types grown and sold as container plants, notably tuberous begonias in full bloom.

Canna   Cannaceae

Growing conditions
Requires good drainage and aeration.
Requires frequent irrigations and ample nutrient to maintain a fast growth rate.

Nutrient requirements
Heavy feeders but nitrogen should be minimised to prevent vegetative growth at the expense of flowers.

Suitable systems
Has been successful in aggregate culture.
Commercial application of cannas in hydroponics is doubtful.

Planting
Propagated by root division.

Special cultural techniques
Trellis and wind protection are needed.

Problems
Very few major problems.

Carnation *Dianthus* sp. Caryophyllaceae

Growing conditions
Good aeration and drainage are critical for optimum cropping.
Optimum temperature for disbuds (or Sims) is 15 to 18 degrees C, and preferably not over 22 degrees C.
Optimum temperature for spray (bunching) carnations is up to 6 degrees higher in summer and 3 degrees higher in winter.
Will tolerate almost freezing temperatures.
Flowering is initiated by both mild to warm temperatures and medium to long days. You need both a good day length and adequate temperatures.
Water requirement can be up to eight times as much in mid-summer compared to mid-winter.
Avoid high humidity.

Nutrient requirements
EC should never exceed 3.5 mS/cm; ideally keep at 2.0 mS/cm.
pH should be around 6.0.
Nutrient solution should be approximately as follows:

Nutrient	ppm	Nutrient	ppm
Nitrogen	170	Iron	1.2
Phosphorus	50	Manganese	0.4
Potassium	245	Copper	0.4
Calcium	160	Zinc	0.2
Magnesium	25	Boron	0.2
		Molybdenum	0.05

Sulphur should not exceed 32 ppm.
Nitrogen should be supplied as nitrate, not as an ammonium salt.
While plants are becoming established nitrogen and calcium requirements are high, but during flowering calcium requirement decreases (up to 30 kg/1000 litre of additional calcium nitrate may be added to the standard nutrient solution over the first few months and gradually be reduced as the plants establish. Established plants should be fed with the standard solution.)

Suitable systems
Rockwool—used commercially in the Netherlands since 1978 and in Australia since 1981.
Rockwool slabs between 10 and 12 cm deep are more successful than shallower slabs. Six to eight drippers should be supplied per square metre of rockwool slab. Set slabs on plastic sheet base with a slight slope for sub-drainage. Plastic sheet can lead to reduced humidity in a greenhouse—in some

Carnations are a common hydroponic crop in rockwool and perlite systems.

Carnation cuttings being propagated in rockwool propagating blocks on a heated bed.

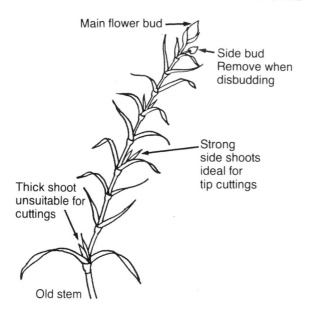

Main flower bud

Side bud
Remove when
disbudding

Strong
side shoots
ideal for
tip cuttings

Thick shoot
unsuitable for
cuttings

Old stem

Pruning carnations to increase flower size and to obtain cutting material.

instances this needs to be countered with routine overhead misting.

Perlite 8–10 cm deep gives excellent results.

Scoria has given good results.

Planting

Use virus-tested cuttings from approved carnation growers. These may be supplied in Growool blocks or perlite tubes. (If in soil-based medium this must be washed off before planting.)

Disbudded carnations (e.g. Sims) are planted at 30–36 plants per square metre.

Spray carnations are commonly planted at 36–48 plants per square metre. A wider spacing improves ventilation and reduces likelihood of disease.

Cropping starts around three months after planting.

Special cultural techniques

Open horizontal mesh 15–20 cm above the medium provides a support system.

Pruning is necessary to stop spindly undesirable growth habits. Pinch out the growing tip on young plants when they reach about 15 cm tall.

Artificial lighting is sometimes used to concentrate flowering period (i.e. you get more flowers over a shorter period, but after that flowering is delayed until the next crop). This is done by lighting at 110 lux from dust till dawn for 4 weeks, usually in mid-winter.

Problems

Hygiene is very important for disease control and consequently crop quality.

Fusarium wilt (*Fusarium oxysporum*) spreads rapidly through irrigation.

Botrytis is sometimes a problem.

Alternaria leaf spot occurs as small purple spots which grow to larger black areas bearing spores.

Viral diseases, mainly transmitted by aphids, are a particularly serious problem reducing cropping in many parts of the world. It is critical to plant only virus-free plants, and to control aphis to prevent healthy plants from becoming infected.

Do not get flower buds or petals wet as this can cause marking.

Flowers which develop at lower temperatures have a tendancy to split.

Flowers developing at higher temperatures develop faster and tend to have weaker stems.

Aphis and mites can be very serious pests. Aphis spread virus and cause distorted growth. Mites cause mottling of the leaves and eventually drying of the foliage.

Thrip and caterpillars can also become a problem.

Harvest and post harvest

For single-flowering varieties the flowers are harvested when the bud has opened fully so that the outer petals are at right angles to the stem and the inner petals are still tightly bunched.

For spray types harvesting occurs when the top three flowers begin expanding and the lower buds are showing colour.

One part boric acid in ten parts water will improve the keeping quality of the flowers by up to one week.

Dipping treatments, based on sodium thiosulphate, that extend the keeping quality of the flowers are also available.

Harvested flowers can be damaged by ethylene. An ethylene-inhibiting chemical is used on flowers which are not sold as soon as they are picked.

Chrysanthemum   Asteraceae

Growing conditions

Requires very good drainage, good aeration and constant moisture in the root zone.

Plants are frost tender.

Needs good light, though shading is sometimes used over summer to provide protection from extreme heat.

Chrysanthemums are a highly marketable crop which have been successfully grown in aggregate systems.

Buds do not form if the period of uninterrupted darkness exceeds 7 hours.

Nutrient requirements
Heavy feeders.
High nitrogen important in the early stages.
Adequate phosphorus at all stages is critical.
Iron deficiency is more likely in a poorly-aerated root zone.
If roots are too wet, high levels of potassium, sodium or nitrogen in the ammonium form will impair the uptake of magnesium, calcium and sulphur.
pH ideally 6.0 to 6.2.

Suitable systems
Aggregate culture has been very successful in sand or perlite.

Planting
Start cuttings in sand, vermiculite or rockwool propagating blocks.
Spacing is dependent on variety with larger varieties spaced up to 70 cm apart.

Special cultural techniques
Pinch out growing tips to cause lateral growths.

Problems
Pests include aphis, mites, whitefly, leaf miners and caterpillars.
Diseases include verticillium wilt, sclerotinia wilt, septoria leaf spot, powdery mildew, botrytis and virus.

Harvest and post harvest
Flowers are harvested when the outer petals have opened, but the inner ones are still expanding.
Sprays are harvested when three or more flowers reach this stage.
The base of the flower stems should be dipped in boiling water for 30 seconds, then placed in buckets of water containing disinfectant such as sodium or calcium hypochlorite.
Flowers protected by a pre-harvest fungicide treatment can be cool stored for up to two weeks at 2–3 degrees C as long as the flowers are dry and the stems are kept in water.

Chryanthemum stock plants should be grown in sterile conditions to ensure disease-free cutting material.

Dahlia   Asteraceae

Growing conditions
Requires better than average moisture when growing fast, with good aeration and drainage.
Plants are frost sensitive.
Optimum temperature range is 16 to 19 degrees C.

Nutrient requirements
Potassium and phosphorus important.
pH 6.0 to 7.0

Suitable systems
Aggregate culture.

Planting
Propagate by cuttings or divisions.

Special cultural techniques
Trellising and wind protection are needed.

Problems
Mildew is more common in hydroponics than soil (plants being more susceptible when growth is very rapid).

Harvest and post harvest
Pick as buds just begin to burst open.

Freesia   Iridaceae

Growing conditions
Corms require 16 degrees C day temperatures (or higher) to commence growing. Once six leaves have formed flowers will begin to develop, and at this stage ideal temperature is 13 degrees C—over 18 degrees C flowering is reduced. After this point, temperatures between 12 and 20 degrees C give optimum growth.
Good lighting is essential for maximum cropping.
Must be cool and moist in the roots while growing.

Nutrient requirements
1.0 mS/cm for the first 2 months then increasing to 2.0 mS/cm.

Suitable systems
Rockwool has been successful in Europe.
Aggregate culture in beds should be successful.

Planting
Plant corms in autumn for spring flowering.

Special cultural techniques
A horizontal trellis for support is necessary.

Problems
Diseases include fusarium wilt, botrytis and virus.
Aphis is perhaps the most serious pest problem because it spreads viral disease.
Thrip and mites can also be serious problems.

Harvest and post harvest
Cut flowers when first bud is starting to open.
You can harvest within 10 to 12 weeks of planting.
Bunch and store at 2 to 4 degrees C.

Gerbera   Asteraceae

Growing conditions
Root aeration is extremely critical.
It is important to maintain active growth over winter to achieve good cropping in the second year.
At temperatures over 18 degrees C it is evergreen, but below 18 it dies back to a dormant root system.
Commercially it is cropped in a heated greenhouse.
It has a high light requirement.

Nutrient requirements
Maintain young plants on an EC of 2.0 mS/cm and increase to 2.5 gradually as plants establish.
pH between 5.0 and 6.5 (pH can drop when plants are producing heavily—if this happens, flush the slab to remove any salt build-up and correct the pH).
pH tends to rise in early spring when there is a lot of leaf growth.

Gerberas growing in aggregate bed. Growool slabs have also been used in commercial systems.

Nutrient solution as follows:

Nutrient	ppm	Nutrient	ppm
Nitrogen	180	Iron	2
(as nitrate		Boron	0.33
Phosphorus	46	Manganese	0.28
Potassium	255	Zinc	0.26
Calcium	160	Copper	0.05
Magnesium	24	Molybdenum	0.05

Sulphur should be no higher than 40.

Suitable systems
Growool slabs are used commercially in Europe. Aggregate culture should also be commercially viable.

Planting
Plants are grown for two seasons then discarded. Propagate by division.
Space 25 to 30 cm between plants.

Special cultural techniques
Horizontal trellis is needed.
Remove one leaf each time you remove a flower to maintain balance between flower and leaf growth. At the end of winter remove all dead or damaged leaves and flower stems.

Problems
A sunny period followed by dull humid weather in summer can cause water problems with the plants losing water at an excessively high rate and requiring extra irrigations, both day and night.
Pest problems include caterpillars, mites, leaf hoppers, mealy bug and other insects.
Disease problems include botrytis, powdery mildew and some blight and rot-causing fungi.

Harvest and post harvest
Flowers must be reasonably mature with stamens in the second ring of disc flowers visible before picking. Pull off flower stalks rather than cutting. Put in a bucket of warm nutrient solution immediately they are picked.

Varieties
Different varieties have different water requirements.

Gladiolus   Iridaceae

Growing conditions
Gladioli grow from a corm. Leaves and roots emerge from the corm in late winter or spring and develop into a plant. The old corm is totally absorbed by the growth, but a new corm forms with many smaller cormlets attached to its bottom. At the end of the growing season, the leaves and roots die back, leaving only the corm and cormlets alive. The corm and cormlets will not regrow until they have undergone a period of dormancy. Over this period, they are susceptible to rotting and hence need to be stored dry. Either remove dormant corms from a hydroponic system or leave the system dry for a period before attempting to start growing a new crop.

Corms formed when the root zone temperatures are above 15 degrees C are more dormant than those that mature when temperatures are cooler. Dormancy has been broken by storage at 5 degrees C for 2 months followed by storage at 20 degrees C.

Adequate light is needed to produce flowers. If light intensity is too low or day lengths too short, flowers will not occur.

Aeration is not as critical as with some crops, though good drainage is essential, particularly for early or late crops.

High humidity around the developing spike can cause fungal diseases and damaged flowers, though this risk is minimal as the flowers are generally picked before opening.

Drier conditions can increase the likelihood of foliage insect problems.

Drier conditions cause earlier flowering.

Nutrient requirements
The most common nutrient deficiencies are iron, boron and copper.
Iron deficiency is indicated by loss of colour between the leaf veins.
Copper deficiency may be indicated by leaves wilting for no apparent reason.
Boron deficiency may be indicated by leaves cracking horizontally.
Nitrogen supplied in the ammonium form increases susceptibility to the fungus *Botrytis gladiolorum*.
Nutrient solutions should preferably supply nitrogen in the nitrate form.
Potash and phosphorus are important.
Because the flower and new corm commence development only 3 to 4 weeks after planting, it is important to provide a strong supply of nutrients early in the growth cycle.
pH should be maintained between 5.5 and 6.5.

Suitable systems
Rockwool and NFT are unsuitable for gladioli.

Aggregate culture is the most suitable technique as it is the only system which provides an appropriate depth and allows corms to be lifted easily for dormant storage at the end of each growing season.

Planting
Plant at a depth of 10 cm.

Special cultural techniques
Some form of trellising is required (either a horizontal mesh, or wires around a row at about 30 cm height).

Problems
Wet, cold conditions promote several fungal diseases including: stromatinia (*Stromatinia gladioli*), botrytis (*Botrytis gladiolorum*) and septoria (*Septoria gladioli*).

In warm conditions gladioli are susceptible to the fungus *Fusarium oxysporum* which attacks both the foliage and the corm.

Virus diseases spread by aphis are one of the most serious pest problems.

Viral infection is indicated by discolouration or blotching of foliage or flowers.

Infected plants cannot be cured and must be removed and burnt to prevent further spread of the disease.

Thrip can be a serious problem in warm weather (temperatures above 20 degrees C), causing silvery streaks on the foliage and subsequent decline in the plant.

Mites, caterpillars and a number of other insects can also be a problem.

Harvest and post harvest
Usually pick between 70 and 140 days from planting.

Harvest when the bottom 2 to 4 flowers on a stem are showing colour. Place in water as soon as picked and store in a cool room between 5 and 7 degrees C.

Iris Iridaceae

Growing conditions
In high humidity, plant rhizomes or bulbs close to the surface of the media. In hot, dry air conditions, plant deeper (2–5 cm below the surface).

Nutrient requirements
Little specific information available for hydroponics.

Suitable systems
Depends on the type of iris. Some types require very little aeration and will grow completely submerged in water, others do not.

Iris laevigata needs to be in extremely wet conditions to thrive. It would be best suited to water culture or perhaps tried in a medium such as 40% vermiculite and 60% perlite.

Iris germanica requires a very well aerated situation. I have grown these successfully in gravel culture with minimal irrigations.

Dutch, Spanish and English irises generally like a drier, better-drained medium than average. These would be best tried in sand or gravel beds.

Planting
Plant bulbs or rhizomes direct into hydroponics.

Special cultural techniques
Some support system is necessary.

Problems
Overwatering will cause bulb or rhizome rot.

Various disease and pest problems include snails and slugs, aphis, thrip, bulb flies, viral diseases, leaf spot, ink spot and iris rust.

Frost can be a problem with some types.

Harvest
Cut when colour begins to appear in the flower.

Varieties
Irises are classified as follows:

1. Bulbous types
a. Xiphiums (Dutch, Spanish, English)
These are very popular as cut flowers worldwide.
b. Early flowering and small Reticulatas
c. Junos varieties

2. Rhizome types
a. Bearded
Have fleshy rhizomes and large wide bladed leaves. These generally prefer warm, dry positions.
b. Beardless
Narrower leaves and smaller fibrous rhizomes. These prefer wet situations.
c. Crested
Thin rhizomes.

Narcissus (Daffodil, Jonquil) Amaryllidaceae

Growing conditions
Require cool conditions with daily maximums not over 21 degrees C and preferably not over 18. Higher temperatures may be tolerated at the end of the growth cycle.

Nutrient requirements
High light intensities can increase iron requirement.

Suitable systems

Aggregate culture is suggested as having the best potential. Narcissus have been grown successfully in 40% perlite and 60% coarse granitic sand.

Planting

Plant at a depth equal to three times the bulb's thickness.

Special cultural techniques

Horizontal trellis for support.

Problems

Pest and disease problems can include mites, bulb flies, slugs, virus, and various fungal rots and leaf-marking diseases.

Harvest and post harvest

Harvest any time from when colour appears in the swollen flower bud (just before or immediately after the flower opens).

Orchids

Orchids are a very large group of plants which vary greatly in appearance and growth requirements. Cymbidiums are the only orchids we know of which have been grown commercially in hydroponics.

Growing conditions

Must have excellent aeration and perfect drainage. Cymbidiums require temperatures between 15 and 25 degrees C, and full light for good growth when young.

Minimum temperature for cymbidiums should be 10 degrees C.

Flowers are initiated during a period of 21 degrees C day temperatures and 14 degrees C night temperatures over summer.

Good ventilation (air movement) around plants is important.

Some types have a semi-dormant period of growth (e.g. dendrobiums) while others, if given optimum conditions, will grow continuously (e.g. cymbidiums).

Nutrient requirements

pH should be around 5.5 for cymbidiums.

Some nitrogen is supplied as ammonium salt to help keep the pH low.

Keep solution at low concentrations of around 0.8 mS/cm or lower.

Sodium and chloride levels must be kept low.

Sulphate content is kept low to stop EC from going too high.

Suitable systems

Traditionally cymbidiums have been grown in peat-based mixes. In Europe there has been increased use of granular rockwool.

Only rockwool or some material with no cation exchange capacity should be used, to minimise salt build-up (see below).

Planting

Grow in individual containers fed by drippers.

As the plants grow in size, the container size and spacing can be increased. Three-year-old plants in 10 litre containers are spaced at 8 plants per square metre; five-year-old plants in 20 litre containers are spaced at 3 plants per square metre.

Problems

Be careful to remove all peat or bark from the roots when transplanting into hydroponics. Residues of such material in a hydroponic medium can attract deposits of salts from nutrient solution. This build-up can eventually reach toxic levels and damage the plant.

Various pests and diseases occur and need to be controlled, including root rots, viruses, mealy bug and aphis.

Harvest and post harvest

Harvest before buds are fully opened.

Cymbidiums will yield up to 90 blooms per square metre per year at five years of age in a good operation.

Orchids have been successfully grown in hydroponic systems, although their particular growth requirements do pose some difficulties.

Roses are grown in perlite and rockwool systems.

Roses should be pruned hard to a basic framework at the end of the flowering season.

Rose *Rosa* sp. Rosaceae

Growing conditions

Good aeration and drainage are vital.

Light intensity must be good, but excessive hot sun will cause scorching.

Ideal temperatures are 15 to 27 degrees C.

Ventilation may be necessary to avoid exceedingly high humidities.

Roses tolerate a very wide range of temperatures and have been grown successfully out of doors from the tropics to some of the coldest temperate regions.

Nutrient requirements

pH 5.5 to 6

EC around 1.5 mS/cm (roses do not tolerate high salt levels).

A suitable nutrient solution would be as follows:

Nutrient	ppm	Nutrient	ppm
Nitrogen	160	Iron	1.4
(as nitrate)		Manganese	0.3
Phosphorus	50	Zinc	0.2
Potassium	230	Boron	0.2
Calcium	160	Molybdenum	0.05
Magnesium	20	Copper	0.04

In more recent times, a more concentrated nutrient solution has been used by some growers who claim better cropping at EC readings of up to 2.5 or higher. Avoid excessive salt build-up (run to waste systems need frequent irrigations to leach out excess of unused salts).

Suitable systems

Perlite.

Granulated rockwool.

Rockwool slabs—used since the mid 1970s in Europe by commercial growers.

The way drainage from the slabs is handled is a critical factor in achieving high productivity. 10 cm deep slabs have proven more successful than 7.5 cm depth.

In Europe, slab heating is frequently used to achieve cropping through winter.

An excess of nutrient solution is normally applied, aiming for a run-off of 15%, or more if conductivity becomes too high.

Over winter, irrigations may be gradually reduced to a level which barely keeps the roots moist while the plants are dormant. Irrigations should return to normal when new season's growth starts.

Planting

Space at least 0.5 m between plants.

Only use budded or grafted plants.

Usually purchased as bare-rooted plants with roots wrapped in sawdust or moss. The best time to buy is early winter. Place orders with wholesale nurseries at least 6 months in advance to be sure of quality plants and the desired varieties.

A young rose crop growing on its own roots in rockwool.

Stocks are relatively easy to grow in rockwool and most aggregate systems.

Special cultural techniques
Regular pruning is essential. Pruning is very heavy in cold climates and light in warm climates.

Problems
Several diseases including black spot, fusarium, pythium, rust, phytophthora and virus etc.
N.B. Fongarid can cause leaf scorch.
Aphis is the most important pest problem.
Other pests can include chafer grubs (on roots), borers, scale, caterpillars, leaf miner, leaf hopper, thrip and red spider mite.
Flower buds sometimes fail to open. Wet or shaded conditions are the most common causes.
Purple to brownish spotting on foliage can be caused by either poor drainage or use of a copper-based spray.

Harvest and post harvest
Harvest swollen buds as colour shows through, before they burst open.
In New Zealand, greenhouse roses grown on a 30 cm grid produce 20 blooms per year per plant (i.e. approximately 220 blooms per square metre). In Israel, with over six months of cropping, yields of 300 blooms per year per square metre have been achieved.

Varieties
Hybrid Tea roses are most commonly used for cut flowers.

Floribundas are also used for cut flowers, but not to the same degree.

Stock   *Matthiola incana*   Cruciferae

Growing conditions
Requires cool temperature, preferably not over 24 degrees C.
Tolerates reasonably moist (but not over-wet) conditions in both air and root environments.
Requires temperatures below 16 degrees C for flowering to be induced.
Grows well in either sun or light shade.

Nutrient requirements
Adequate calcium and potassium are important.
pH 6.0 to 7.0

Suitable systems
Relatively easy to grow in rockwool or most aggregate systems.

Planting
Sow seed direct or transplant seedlings started in vermiculite, perlite or rockwool propagating blocks.

Problems
Aphis can become a problem on mature plants. Seedlings are susceptible to fungal diseases if they become too wet.

Harvest and post harvest
Store at 10 degrees C or a little lower after harvest.

15 Other Plants in Hydroponics

Indoor Plants

African violet *Saintpaulia* sp. Gesneriaceae

Growing conditions
Minimum temperature of 15 degrees C, a relatively even temperature with no cold draughts or other sudden temperature changes.
Bright light (day length of 16 hours or more is needed for flowering).
High humidity.

Nutrient requirements
Maintain a lower EC than many other plants.
pH 6.0 to 7.0

African violet capillary fed from reservoir below pot.

Suitable systems
Self-watering pots with aggregate are very successful.
50/50 sand and perlite, expanded clay and scoria have been successful.

Planting
Propagates readily from leaf cuttings in 40% perlite, and 60% coarse granitic sand.
Has potential to sell as a flowering container plant growing in a hydroponic pot.

Special cultural techniques
Remove dead flowers and older marked leaves.
Do not allow water to get on the foliage.

Problems
Markings on leaves are commonly caused by adverse environmental conditions.
Fungal diseases include crown rot (occurs with overwatering), botrytis and powdery mildew (which occur when leaves are sprayed with mist).
Pest problems include whitefly, mealy bug and mites.

Anthurium Araceae

Growing conditions
Minimum temperature of 15 degrees C, optimum growth is between 18 and 21 degrees C.
Bright light is required in winter but summer shading may be necessary.
Humidity is important (misting helps in dry climates).
Root zone temperature and moisture must be

maintained at constant levels, hence a freely draining medium with good insulation properties is best.

Nutrient requirements
pH 5.0 to 6.0

Suitable systems
Has been grown successfully in high quality peat. Perlite or mixtures of sand with vermiculite or perlite should be suitable in self-watering pots. Be careful not to use a medium which becomes too wet though.
Can be grown for commercial sale as a container plant or a cut flower.

Planting
Propagated by division when temperatures are around 21 degrees C.

Special cultural techniques
Remove spent flowers or damaged leaves.

Problems
Low humidity leads to poor flowering, brown leaf tips and curled leaves.
Low temperature can cause yellowing of foliage.
Pests can include mealy bug, aphis, scale.
Fungal diseases can rot roots in over-wet conditions.

Harvest and post harvest
If grown as a cut flower, flowers are cut when 75% open, stood in a preservative solution and stored at 13 degrees C. They will keep up to four weeks with regular changes to the solution.

Aphelandra   Acanthaceae

Growing conditions
Minimum temperature of 12 degrees C, a preferred temperature of 18 degrees C and high humidity, bright light but not direct sunlight, constant moisture and good aeration.

Nutrient requirements
Heavy feeders.
pH 5.0 to 6.0

Suitable systems
Aggregate culture in 50 to 70% sand mixed with peat, vermiculite or perlite, or in pure perlite, expanded clay or scoria.

Planting
Propagate by 8 cm tip cuttings in late spring.

Special cultural techniques
Minimise watering at lower temperatures when growth slows to prevent root rots.

Problems
Pests include aphis and mealy bug.

Bromeliads   Bromeliaceae

Growing conditions
Most will tolerate temperatures as low as 9 degrees C, some will tolerate much lower temperatures, but not frost.
High temperatures (over 25 degrees C) are required to initiate flowering.
Bright light is important, but not direct sunlight.

Nutrient requirements
Nutrient requirements are relatively low.
pH 5.0 to 7.5

Suitable systems
Most types of aggregate culture are successful.

Planting
Propagate from offset division.

Special cultural techniques
Remove dead flowers and leaves.

Problems
Bromeliads have few problems.

Caladium   Araceae

Growing conditions
Temperatures should never be below 15 and preferably always above 21 degrees C.
Moderate light requirement (no direct sunlight).
High humidity, good drainage and even root zone temperature.

Nutrient requirements
pH 6.0 to 7.5

Suitable systems
Well-draining, well-insulated aggregate media such as perlite would probably be best.

Planting
Plant tubers early spring.
Propagate by removing developing tubers from parent plant.

Special cultural techniques
As foliage dies back in autumn, lift tuber, trim off foliage and roots and store at 15 degrees C until early spring.

Problems
Several fungal and insect problems can occur.
Many of these are more likely to become serious when the plant is weakened by adverse environmental conditions.

Dieffenbachia   Araceae

Growing conditions
Temperature never below 15 degrees C, bright light in winter but partial shade in summer, high humidity and warmth are essential for best results.
Root environment should be constantly moist and well aerated.

Nutrient requirements
High nitrogen requirement.
pH 5.0 to 6.0

Suitable systems
Aggregate and water culture have been successful.

Planting
Propagate by tip or stem cuttings.

Problems
Pests include scale and spider mites.
Excess water can cause stems to rot or discolour.
Cool temperatures or excess light can cause yellowing of foliage.

Dracaena   Agavaceae

Growing conditions
Temperature preferably not below 13 degrees C, ideally 18 to 24 degrees C.
High humidity, light summer shading and constant moisture in the root zone are important.

Nutrient requirements
pH 5.0 to 6.0

Suitable systems
Most types of aggregate culture should be successful. A heavier medium (e.g. scoria or expanded clay) may be preferable to give better anchorage.

Planting
Propagated by stem cuttings.

Special cultural techniques
Some form of suport may be needed, particularly in light-weight media.

Problems
Too much water or excessive cold are the main reasons for death.
Several pests and diseases can occur.

Ferns

Growing conditions
Ferns vary greatly in temperature requirements according to variety.
Most grow well between 16 and 21 degrees C.

Maidenhair fern in Decor Waterwell pot. Nutrient solution is fed by capillary action from a reservoir below pot.

Most respond to some light (but not bright), prefer high humidity and constant moisture in the root zone.

Nutrient requirements
pH requirement varies but most do well at 6.0.

Suitable systems
Luwasa self-watering pots with expanded clay aggregate have been used successfully.
Perlite and peat have been successful with many ferns.

Special cultural techniques
Many ferns are deciduous and their foliage will die off for a period of the year. These are more susceptible to root-rot fungi if kept too moist when devoid of foliage.

Problems
Many pest and disease problems occur, including scale, mealy bug, caterpillars, aphis, snails etc.

Ficus   Moraceae

Growing conditions
While many are relatively cold tolerant, most are best kept at temperatures above 15 degrees C.
Relatively low water requirements but high humidity is preferable.

Ficus elastica needs a heavy aggregate such as scoria, gravel or expanded clay.

Nutrient requirements
pH 5.5 to 6.0

Suitable systems
Best in a heavy aggregate such as gravel, scoria or expanded clay.

Planting
Propagate by cuttings or layering.

Problems
Mites thrive in low humidity. Scale can also be a problem.
Excess water can lead to fungal root and stem rots.

Impatiens

Growing conditions
Bright light but not hot direct light in summer.
Ideally temperatures around 24 degrees C and preferably never below 12 degrees C.
High humidity, moderate water levels and reasonable aeration in the root zone.

Nutrient requirements
pH 5.5 to 6.5

Suitable systems
Most aggregate systems are suitable.

Planting
Propagate by cuttings or seed.

Special cultural techniques
Remove dead flowers.
Prune back hard annually, just before new season's growth starts.

Problems
Excess water can result in rots developing.
Pests include thrip, aphis and mealy bug.

Monstera Araceae

Growing conditions
Ideally 21 degrees C though relatively cold tolerant (but not frost tolerant).
Needs well-aerated freely-draining root environment which is never too wet.
High humidity is desirable but not necessary.

Nutrient requirements
pH 5.0 to 6.0

Suitable systems
Heavier coarse aggregates are best for both maintaining preferred moisture levels and giving good anchorage.

Planting
Propagate by layers or cuttings.

Problems
Relatively few except excess water in the root environment.
Mites and mealy bug can occur.

Palms Palmaceae

Growing conditions
Ideal temperature varies according to variety though most prefer over 15 degrees C, ideally over 20 degrees C.
Good light is important, though some shading may be needed in summer.
Excellent drainage is important.

Nutrient requirements
Though they respond to high levels of feeding, it has been shown this increases the rate of metabolism and, in the case of palms, shortens the period they can be kept indoors.
pH 6.0 to 7.5

Suitable systems
Scoria, gravel, sand or expanded clay are most likely to suit.

Planting
Propagates slowly (sometimes several years to germinate) from seed.

Special cultural techniques
Need to be rejuvenated in a greenhouse or shadehouse every 1 to 3 years.

Problems
Pests can include mealy bug, mites and scale.

Herbs

References: *Herb Grower and Marketer*, Spring issue, 1987
The Potential of Herbs as a Cash Crop by Miller, *Acres*, 1985

Basil (Sweet)   *Ocimum basilicum*   Lamiaceae

Basil foliage is sold as a fresh-cut herb for culinary use or processed for the oil which is used in cosmetics, soaps and processed foods.

Growing conditions
Ideally around 20–24 degrees C.
Continually moist but well-aerated root environment.
Needs good light conditions, although some shade may be needed in summer.

Nutrient requirements
pH 5.5 to 6.5

Suitable systems
Has been successful in NFT (7–8 cm channels), scoria and sand/peat.
Should be successful in rockwool.

Planting
Seed germinates in 4 to 7 days at 21 degrees C in rockwool cubes or perlite.
Plant out at 20 cm spacings in early spring.

Special cultural techniques
Trellis support is needed.

Problems
Vigorous roots can clog NFT channels after a while.

Harvest and post harvest
Harvest before flowering starts.
For the first harvest remove tips with one to two nodes. Side shoots will develop and a second harvest can be made about a month later. Further harvests can be made until mid-autumn when the crop is removed.

Basil can be grown in NFT, scoria and sand/peat systems.

Harvest in the morning when cool and place immediately in cool place at around 5 degrees C.

Lemon balm   *Melissa officinalis*   Lamiaceae

Though not grown widely as a commercial crop, the lemon-flavoured foliage is an excellent lemon substitute as a tea or in food processing.

Growing conditions
Will take full sun but prefers some shading, dry air environment is preferable.

Nutrient requirements
pH 5.5 to 6.5 Will not grow at pH below 4.5

Suitable systems
Aggregate culture, NFT or rockwool should all succeed.

Planting
Propagates easily from seed or root division in late winter or early spring.
Space at 30–40 cm.

Special cultural techniques
Trellising and wind protection are necessary.

Problems
Foliage can turn brown if it gets wet at night.
There are relatively few pest or disease problems. White fly and aphis have occurred though.

Harvest and post harvest
Harvest in cool time of day and package in plastic to reduce moisture loss.

Keep out of direct sunlight and at a low temperature to reduce condensation (which promotes fungal problems).

Marjoram *Origanum majorana* Lamiaceae

Sold as dried leaves for culinary purposes, or extracted oil which is used in cosmetics and foods. Oregano which is closely related (and grown similarly) is prefered for use in herbal medicines.

Growing conditions
Must be well aerated but constantly moist around the roots.

Nutrient requirements
pH ideally 6.0, never below 5.0.

Suitable systems
NFT has been successful.
Sand, gravel, perlite and rockwool are recommended also.

Planting
Seed germinates easily in about a week at 20 degrees C.

Problems
Aphis may be a problem.

Harvest and post harvest
Make the first cut when 'ball'-like growths appear on the stems. Cut back to within 3 cm of the base. The regrowth which occurs generally gives the best crop. Further harvests can also be made.
Most of the oils are retained in dried leaves, though they should be stored in air tight containers and kept in the dark.

Mint *Mentha* sp. Lamiaceae

Several species are grown commercially, mainly for oil production. Peppermint which yields menthol is the most widely grown. Though generally cultivated in soil, there may be potential for hydroponic farming.

Growing conditions
Adapts well to wet conditions with medium aeration, grows well at mild temperatures (i.e. 15 to 20 degrees C).

Nutrient requirements
pH 6.5 to 7.0 Will not grow at a pH level below 4.5.

Suitable systems
NFT has been very successful.

Planting
Plant cuttings or divisions in late winter.

Problems
Common pests include cutworms, caterpillar, flea beetle, aphis, mites and root weevils.
Verticillium wilt can also be a problem.
Vigorous root system can block NFT channels. Plants should be replaced periodically.

Harvest and post harvest
Mint cut for fresh market should be kept cool (5 degrees C), out of the sun, and not bruised at all (this accelerates fungal damage).
Store at 95% humidity or wrap to prevent moisture loss. Keep out of direct sun.

Parsley *see* vegetable chapter.

Rosemary *Rosmarinus officinalis* Lamiaceae

Growing conditions
Well-aerated mildly-moist (never saturated but never dry) root environment.
Temperatures below –2 degrees C will cause death; prefers full sun or slight shade.

Nutrient requirements
pH 5.5 to 6.0

Suitable systems
Has been successful in NFT.
Will grow in sand, gravel or perlite.

Planting
Space at 0.5 m intervals.

Problems
Rosemary has few problems.

Harvest and post harvest
Foliage is marketed for use fresh or dried for culinary purposes.
Oil is a highly marketable commodity.

Sage *Salvia officinalis* Lamiaceae

Growing conditions
Requires good light conditions.
Requires excellent aeration but also constant moisture (it will die if soil around roots is dry). Ideally tempertures should be between 18 and 24 degrees C.

Nutrient requirements
Will not grow at a pH below 4.0.
pH 5.5 to 6.5

Suitable systems
Has been successful in NFT.
Is likely to grow best in coarse aggregate.

Planting
Propagate from seed or cuttings.
Space 30 to 50 cm apart.

Special cultural techniques
Wind protection is important and trellising may be beneficial.

Problems
There are few problems, though aphis infestations occasionally occur.

Harvest and post harvest
Leaves are harvested and sold fresh or dried. Oil is extracted commercially.

Thyme *Thymus vulgaris* Lamiaceae

Growing conditions
Ideal temperature is 20 to 24 degrees C.
Media should be well drained but always moist. Full sun is desirable though shading may be beneficial to control temperature in summer.

Nutrient requirements
pH 5.5 to 7.0 Will not grow at a pH below 4.5

Suitable systems
There has been difficulty with NFT.
Sand, gravel or rockwool may be more successful.

Planting
Depending on variety, usually space at 15 to 25 cm.

Problems
Few pests and diseases.
Occasionally aphis is a problem.

Harvest and post harvest
Cut foliage back hard periodically, harvest regrowth periodically.

Grass

Fodder

Grass and other fodder crops for animals have been grown successfully in hydroponic installations. Common agricultural practice involves grazing animals in fresh grass in the warmer months and feeding them with dry, cut fodder in the cooler months. A distinct advantage of hydroponic fodder is that it can be produced year round giving animals fresh green food over winter.

The protein content of some fodder varieties grown hydroponically is significantly higher than when the same plants are grown in soil. Farmers in several countries have claimed an increase in milk yields from cows fed on hydroponic fodder.

Depending on the animal, between 5 and 10 kg of fresh fodder will be eaten per animal per day.

Growing conditions
Optimum temperature depends on variety, but usually around 20 to 24 degrees C.
Good light intensity is also important.

Nutrient requirements
Most grasses prefer a pH of around 6.0

Suitable systems
NFT—Using wide channels (20-30 cm), a sheet of water-absorbant paper is laid in the channel base to give a capillary-matting effect. Seed is sown on the sheet. The solution flow should be continuous but not so strong that it moves the seed. The top of the channel remains exposed to light. Once the seed has germinated and grown into the paper, the flow rate can be increased (the roots and grass blades will restrict the water flow requiring an increasingly stronger flow rate).
Plants can be recut later for more fodder. Progressive cropping of the same plants is an option, however disease can build up and flow become restricted to the point where a fresh sowing becomes necessary.
Peat bed—A shallow bed of peat can be seeded and sub-irrigated.
Plants can be cut or lifted as a matted sheet for use.
Other methods—Most other types of aggregate bed can be used, though the plants must be cut. Be careful not to get media such as perlite or vermiculite mixed with fodder as these materials can harm animals which eat them.

Special cultural techniques
Multi level systems—Fodder can be grown in several layers on racks in a shed or greenhouse with the use of artificial lights (N.B. You must use the proper wavelength light source e.g. Grolites.)

Problems
If using paper as a capillary mat be sure it doesn't contain newsprint or any other source of phytotoxic chemicals.

Varieties
The following have been grown successfully in hydroponics: oats, wheat, rye, barley, sorghum.

Chitted seed for turf

Chitted seed is pre-germinated lawn seed. Hydroponic systems can be used to commence germination prior to sowing.

This process usually takes up to one week. Seed is removed from the system and sown when roots have emerged but before cotyledons have fully opened on most seeds.

Growing conditions
Depend on grass variety, but generally as for forage crops.

Nutrient requirements
pH 6.0
Nutrient solution is not needed as the seed has a store of food.

Suitable systems
Sprinkle a thin layer of peat, perlite or vermiculite on black plastic sheets on the floor of a greenhouse in winter. Mix in grass seed. Water until thoroughly moist. Keep wet but not overwatered for 5 to 7 days then remove and sow the seed as you would do normally for a lawn.

Planting
The area can be aerated then chitted seed raked into the holes created by the aerator.
Seed can be spread then covered with a layer of topsoil.

Problems
Rough handling can damage seed.
Chitted seed is extremely susceptible to drying out and dying within the first week following planting. It must be kept well watered.

Propagation/Nursery Production

Hydroponics has been used commercially for plant propagation in several places. Aeroponics, rockwool propagation blocks, perlite and gravel culture have all been successfully used for striking cuttings and raising plants for selling bare rooted (e.g. perennials, indoor plants, woody shrubs etc).

Other Crops

Sholto Douglas (in *Advanced Guide to Hydroponics*) suggests the following are well suited to propagating in hydroponics: cocoa (*Theobroma cacao*), coffee (*Coffea arabica*), sugar cane (*Saccharum officinarum*), rubber (*Hevea brasiliensis*), tea (*Camellia thea*) and tobacco (*Nicotiana tabacum*).

He gives specific recommendations and claims that frequently the quality of young plants produced is far better when they are started in hydroponic culture.

PART 3

16   Managing a Commercial Hydroponics Farm

Growing plants in hydroponics is one thing, but operating a viable hydroponic farm is altogether another.

Commercial hydroponics is not just about setting up and operating hydroponic systems. If you are to be successful and run a viable operation you must also:

1. Select the right crops to grow
2. Have a workable physical layout
3. Manage your staff and finances properly
4. Market your produce properly.

Deciding What to Grow

When deciding what plants to grow, consider the following:

1. Ease of propagation/cost of transplants
What will it cost to get your initial plants (in time *or* money)?
If you plan to propagate yourself: are they very easy to propagate, or difficult?
Are the plants readily available?
Is the recommended planting time the same as the time of year you plan to start your operation?

2. How easy are these plants to grow?
Do you (or your staff) have the expertise to grow these varieties?
Difficult plants may be more costly to grow, and

more risky to get a profit from, unless you have better than average skills.

3. How long will the crop take to grow?
Some plants produce a crop ready to sell within months, others take many years.

4. Suitability to your facilities
Do you have the right buildings, equipment and other facilities to grow the particular plants under consideration?
Do you have the money and space to provide those facilities?

5. Suitability of climate
What plants are most suitable to grow in your climate?
It is always more efficient to work with the environment rather than trying to recreate different environments.

6. Are other competent growers already producing the crop you would prefer to grow? Can you establish a share of that market?

7. Distance from potential markets
Transport is costly, and can be risky.
What other alternatives are available?

8. Are profits (in addition to wages) likely to be an adequate or reasonable return on your investment in terms of time and money?

9. Your staff's skills
Don't try to do what you are not skilled to do. Someone with better skills will probably do it better and cheaper.

Crop Scheduling

Throughout the life of any crop, you will need to perform a number of operations. It is often helpful to break down the growing period into weeks, designating the tasks which are to be undertaken each week. (Obviously the actual time of carrying out any task will vary a little according to the changes in the weather and different varieties of plant etc.)

Example of a simple flow chart for growing lettuce

Week 1   Sow seed in 75% sand and 25% peat and place in greenhouse.
Week 2   Check for germination. Keep well watered.
Week 3   Check for damping off, thin out if necessary. Spray fungicide if necessary.
Week 4   Plant seedlings into NFT channels.
Spray with insecticide (malathion) for caterpillars etc.
Feed with high nitrogen fertiliser.
Week 5   Check for insect and fungal problems. Remove affected leaves and plants, or spray.
Week 6   Treat with fungicide.
Week 7   Check for disease, insect damage and nutrient deficiencies.
Week 9   Harvest.

Obviously some crops involve more work— pruning, changing nutrient solutions, shading, temperature control, staking etc. Any such tasks should be included in a flow chart.

This type of analysis of the crop's life will help you plan your production.

Standards

A hydroponic farm, like any business, must set and adhere to certain standards if it is going to operate profitably. These standards can be broken down into three main groups:

1. Cost efficiency standards
2. Quality standards
3. Quantity standards.

Cost Efficiency

There must be a sound relationship between cost of production and sales price. Both of these monetary figures must be constantly monitored and maintained at an acceptable level so as to ensure profitability in the business.

Cost of production + profit = Sales price

If the cost of production gets too high, then profit will decrease. In such a situation, the sales price must be increased, or else the profit figure can become a minus amount (i.e. you might be losing money rather than making it).

In order to control your cost effectiveness, you must make it your business to know (and control) all factors which influence cost of production.

Cost of production is influenced by the following factors:

• Cost of site (lease/rent value)
• Cost of site services (power, gas, water, insurance, rates etc.)
• Cost of materials (soil, pots, fertilisers etc.)
• Cost of unsold produce—a certain proportion may be lost, may die, or may just become unsaleable. (Some horticultural businesses budget for as much as 30% of stock being thrown away.)
• Labour costs (be sure to include your own time as well as employees').
• Advertising promotion (printing, advertising in magazines etc.)
• Selling costs (transportation, invoicing etc.)
• Taxation (don't forget payroll tax, income tax etc.).

Profit

This figure should be over and above money which you earn as wages. If you are only working for wages (with no profit), then you would be better off putting your money into some different form of investment and going to work for someone else.

Profit should be greater than the interest rate which you could get by investing your money elsewhere. Profit should normally be at least 15-20%. In horticultural businesses the profit margin can vary greatly from crop to crop and year to year. You will find that profit will be very low (possibly nothing) some years, and high other years.

The profit must be viewed in terms of an average over several years. New operations should always have sufficient liquidity to carry them over if they have a couple of bad seasons before some good seasons come along.

Sales price

The figure which produce is sold for can vary considerably. This can be due to such factors as overall economic conditions, general availability of the product you are selling, and consumer demand.

Quality Standards

The following factors are of concern when considering produce quality:

- General appearance of vigour or health such as markings or lack of markings on produce (e.g. disease, rot, bruising etc).
- Taste or smell (e.g. how sweet or bitter).
- Freshness (i.e. the quicker you can sell it after harvest, the better the quality will be considered).

Quantity Standards

Commercial production must achieve certain standards in terms of the quantity of produce being harvested, its weight and the size of each individual unit (e.g. how many strawberries will you pick per year per square metre, and how big will each strawberry be).

- For some crops, the size is not critical but the number is. (e.g. Orchids are sold on the number of flowers. A slightly smaller or larger flower will not make a great deal of difference to the cost).
- For other crops weight is critical, but size doesn't matter. (e.g. Beans are sold by the kilogram, irrespective of whether they are large or small beans).
- For other crops size and weight are both important. (e.g. Strawberries are sold by the kilogram, but large ones are sold at a different rate from small ones.)

Farm Layout

A well laid-out farm will be more efficient, less costly to operate in terms of manpower and cost, and will return greater profits. It is essential that equipment, materials and people are able to move easily from one area to another. To achieve this you should do the following:

1. Study the work operations which take place.
2. Identify movements which occur the most (e.g. people and equipment will move from the store room to the nutrient tanks more commonly than from the nutrient tanks to the packing sheds).
3. Design the farm in a way that makes movement easiest along the paths which are used the most (e.g. nutrient tanks should be closer to the store than to the packing sheds).

There are three aspects to work carried out on any hydroponics farm: growing, harvesting and marketing.

These three areas should be segregated as much as possible.

Good layout decisions based on the above principles are as follows:

- Tools, equipment and chemicals used in production should be kept away from the marketing side of the operation.
- Delivery vehicles should have easy access to the property, and deliveries should be able to be made as close as possible to store rooms or sheds.
- Delivery vans, staff cars and vehicles transporting produce should have restricted access to the property. In general these vehicles not only take up space, but they can bring disease onto the property, as well as being a security problem. Consequently, loading and unloading bays are best situated close to the front of the property.
- Post-harvest operations including sorting, grading, packing and storage should be done under cover to protect produce, and should be located within easy reach of the crop. It should be possible to move produce into this area quickly and easily after harvest.
- Concrete or asphalt pathways and floors should be used in areas where wheeled tools or equipment are to be used, or areas which must remain clean (e.g. A path leading to a greenhouse should preferably be sealed to keep shoes clean and reduce the chance of disease being carried into the house).
- Potentially dangerous situations should not be allowed (e.g. objects protruding into work areas and access tracks—overhead objects should not be so low as to restrict clear access).

Design of a Store

A storeroom or storage shed must be accessible from other parts of the farm, secure, and have an interior design which allows for easy access to stores.

- Both expensive and dangerous items can be stored

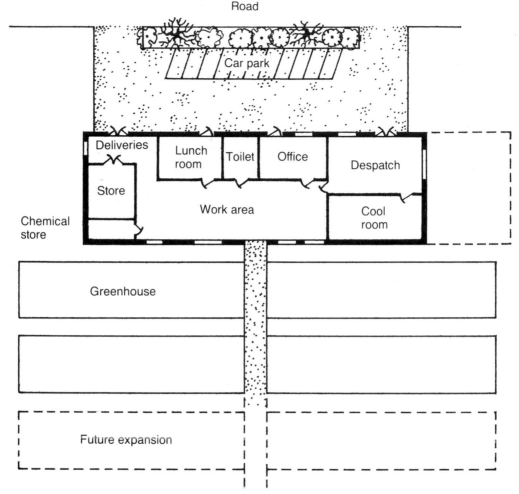

Well designed hydroponic farm

Features which make this a good design include:

- Access to vehicles and visitors is restricted to the front of the property.
- Delivery and despatch areas are easily accessible to trucks (little turning is required).
- Chemical store is lockable, separate from main store and away from eating area (i.e. lunch room).
- Cool room where harvest is stored is separated from other work areas (this maintains better hygiene).
- Greenhouse growing areas are easily accessible via a central pathway which is close to both the general work area and the despatch/cool room area.
- The service building and greenhouses are placed so that future expansion of both areas would be simple with minimal disruption of day to day business.

on a farm. The store should be securely locked and there should be a limit on staff who have free access.

- Doors of small stores should open out allowing better access inside.
- Pesticides or other dangerous chemicals should be stored in a separate lock-up cupboard or room. This is often required by law. There may also be legal obligations to place danger signs on such storage areas.
- It is preferable that all equipment and materials, where practical, be stored on racks or shelves, off the ground (for cleanliness), and properly labelled where necessary.

Marketing Your Produce

Marketing takes in everything involved in the process of taking your produce to the final customer. If you are to market your produce well, you need

to understand all the steps in this process, and make sure each step is done as well as possible.
Typical steps in marketing are:

- Packaging and storing the produce—this affects its attractiveness to potential buyers and its longevity.
- Transporting the produce
- Promoting the produce
- Selling.

Considering Your Markets

Hydroponic produce, whether fruit, vegetables or cut flowers, is generally sold through one of the following:

1. Direct sales to the public
(E.g. from the packing shed on your property, or from a roadside stall.) Some growers have supplemented their income by tapping the tourist market and catering in other ways to people visiting their property. It may be very viable to consider setting up conducted tours of a hydroponic farm together with direct sales of produce, and perhaps a shop selling souvenirs, refreshments etc.
Some such operations may involve 'pick your own' sales where the public pays a bargain price for what they pick themselves. This has been done commercially with NFT strawberries in Victoria.

2. Sales through major markets
Major cities operate fruit, vegetable and cut-flower markets through which growers sell produce to shopkeepers. You can hire a stand or sell through an agent (who generally takes a commission) at such markets.

3. Selling direct to retail outlets
It may be viable for you to do your own distribution with some crops, and if you are big enough to make it worthwhile. Distribution can be expensive and time consuming though, and should not be tackled lightly.

4. Contract growing
Some companies will contract produce to be grown for processing in factories. Generally the price paid for produce is predetermined, limiting the amount of profit which the grower may make, but giving a guaranteed sale.

Chrysanthemums bunched and wrapped in cellophane for sale.

Daffodils on display at trade show—bulb orders are taken from this display.

Market Research

One of the major keys to success in any business is to 'know your market'. If you know that there is demand for what you are planning to grow, and if you can pinpoint where that demand is, your chances of success will increase greatly (not to mention the sleepless nights you will save). So one of the most important things you can do before growing any new crop is to thoroughly research the market.

Successful marketing depends upon knowing the people/groups you are marketing to—what they want, how they are likely to react to your product, what they will spend money on etc.

When the market place is understood, you can then follow the steps below to achieve successful marketing:

1. Set realistic marketing goals
2. Provide structures for reaching those goals
3. Assess the results of marketing efforts and modify your approaches accordingly.

Market research involves all those activities which help management reach marketing decisions. It attempts to make the unknown known; and in most instances, largely succeeds.

Steps involved in market research

1. Define the problem—what information is required?
(e.g. how can I increase sales by 10%? . . . or Should I change the way I distribute my produce?)
2. Conduct an investigation.
Examine past records which relate to the problem. Speak with people in the know, who might help with this problem. Try to find any relevant information which has been published (e.g. in trade magazines, bureau of statistics etc).
3. If more information is required, you may decide to survey the customers (or potential customers). Note: this involves significantly more cost.
4. If the problem is still beyond you, you may employ a professional market research firm to handle it.

Gathering information

There are various ways you can obtain information about the market. After considering the possible marketing avenues (e.g. direct sales to the public, selling through major markets, contract growing etc.), and the type of produce you might grow; you should next try to find out all you can about the market you are considering. Get to know the details of how that market operates, what your chances might be of breaking in to that market and how strong that market is.

This information can be gathered in three main ways: asking questions, observing people or referring to literature.

1. Literature

Magazines, newspapers and books are a great source of information. They can give a very good indication of what markets are most viable; however, literature is not always up to date. Material published today may have been written months or years ago, and may not be an accurate reflection of the situation.

Newspapers and monthly magazines are generally better than quarterly journals or books.

2. Asking people (i.e. surveys)

Formal or informal, surveys can tell you a lot about a market. Surveys are relatively inexpensive and adaptable to a wide variety of situations. Questions are asked through personal interviews, mail questionnaires, telephone interviews etc.
• Mail and telephone surveys are less expensive.
• Telephone surveys produce quickest results.
• Personal interviews are the most accurate.

3. Watching people

Much can be learnt by observing people in the market place. Visit a fruit or flower shop and watch what they buy, what produce they are attracted to, and how they buy.

This involves observing reactions when something is presented to people. Some growers get excellent feedback from the public when they put on a promotional display at an agricultural or trade show.

The main disadvantage is that observations may not be accurate.

What do you need to research

In any business, success is determined by a combination of many factors, and different factors are relevant in different situations. However, the following areas are commonly researched:

• Progressive or backward (Is the market for your proposed produce expanding or contracting?)

Retailing—presentation is vital! Colour at the front of the shop attracts!

Selling from a roadside stall.

- Is the competition helpful and courteous to customers . . . or not?
- Does the competition give quick and efficient service?
- Is the produce you have in mind advertised/promoted well or poorly in the marketplace?
- Is the produce you are considering inexpensive or expensive?

How to sell successfully

Whether you sell direct to the public or only deal with contractors or agents, you will find some basic sales skills can be invaluable. Often your ability to sell is the difference between a successful hydroponic business and financial disaster. When you negotiate a sale, be prepared and make sure you know the following:

- Details of what you are selling; its attributes, its competition, its negative points (and how to counteract these).
- Where and how to find the product/brochures/catalogues/order forms . . . or anything else relating to the sale.
- The prices to charge and terms of sale.
- Procedure for making a sale (including using cash register, filling out order book, writing receipt etc).
- Company policies (on returns, damaged goods etc).
- How to package or deliver goods or services (e.g. wrapping, directing other staff to deliver service or goods etc).
- How to keep records in order.
- How to maintain order and tidiness in sales area/equipment etc.

A good salesperson should possess the following characteristics:

- A good appearance
- A pleasant personality
- Courtesy and tact
- Ability to enjoy selling
- A basic understanding of human nature (practical not theoretical—ability to read people's body language etc).

Key rules every salesperson should follow

- Research your customer and product first. (You need to know both the customer and the product before you attempt to sell.)
- Find out everything your customer needs to buy before you start dealing.
- Highlight the benefits of a product rather than the features. (Tell the customer what it can do for him personally . . . don't tell him what is great and unique about the product if it is not relevant to him in particular.)
- If there are objections, play it cool and try to determine very specifically what they are—once you narrow down the objection, put it into perspective by showing something about the product which compensates for that objection (e.g. Yes it is expensive—but it will sell better). Don't make it seem as if you have won a point.
- Always keep control of the conversation—don't let yourself get into a defensive position. This is done by asking questions when the customer starts to take the offensive.
- Do not talk while showing the product. Show them, then stop and talk, stop talking while you show them again . . . etc.
- Handle produce with respect.
- Get the customer to try out the product (e.g. give him a strawberry to eat or a flower to smell).
- If you need to, use the phone or calculator to buy thinking time (excuse yourself to make a phone call or calculate some figures).
- Try to close the sale—ask for an order at the appropriate time, when the customer seems to be in a state of mind where he/she is likely to buy. (Many a good sale is lost because the salesman doesn't close the deal when he has the chance. Once you and the customer part ways, the chances of getting back together to finalise the deal are greatly reduced).
- Remember that fulfilling the customer's needs is more important than improving your own knowledge or sales technique.
- Do not forget that the customer is always right—without him you are not going to remain in business.

Directory

The following contacts are from a list maintained and regularly updated by staff of the Australian Horticultural Correspondence School. If you wish to change or add to information on this list please contact the school. Up to date copies of the list can be obtained from the school. Write to: The Australian Horticultural Correspondence School 264 Swansea Rd, Lilydale, Victoria, Australia, 3140.

Courses

Two home study courses, 'Hydroponics' and 'Advanced Hydroponics', have been conducted by the Australian Horticultural Correspondence School since the early 1980s. These courses were thoroughly revised and updated in early 1990.

'Hydroponics' is an introductory course taking around 100 hours to complete. 'Advanced Hydroponics' is a commercially oriented course aimed at the experienced grower, or at least a knowledgeable amateur. It takes between 120 and 150 hours to complete.

A new course, the Certificate in Horticultural Technology (Hydroponics), involves around 400 to 500 hours of study, over thirty lessons. Approximately half the course is devoted to hydroponics. Systems dealt with include aggregate culture, NFT, rockwool and aeroponics. The remainder of the course covers such subjects as plant physiology and growth requirements, nutrition, propagation, tissue culture, growth control equipment (ie: heating, cooling, light controls, CO_2 enrichments, etc.), greenhouses, shadehouses, computer applications, irrigation, pest and disease control, growth regulators, etc.

The school conducts more than 100 other correspondence courses including such subjects as cut flower growing, commercial vegetable growing, marketing and certificates and diplomas in horticulture and business. These courses can be taken by correspondence from any part of the world. Further Details: AHCS, 264 Swansea Rd, Lilydale, Australia 3140.

Societies

International Society of Soilless
  Culture
Headquarters: PO Box 52, 6700
  AB Wageningen, The
  Netherlands
Australian contact: Keith Maxwell,
  30 Sophia Cres, North Rocks,
  2151

Australian Hydroponics
  Association Inc.
c/- PO Box 823, Murwillumbah,
  NSW, 2484
Hydroponic Society of Victoria
136 Heathmont Road, Heathmont,
  3135. Ph (03) 729 5170
Hydroponics Section of the Royal
  Horticultural Society of NSW
GPO Box 4728, Sydney, 2001

Cairns Hydroponic Society
Att: William Meehan
9 Marrett St, Stratford, 4870

Darwin Hydroponic Society
Att: Bryan Mund
60 Hudson-Fysh Ave, Darwin,
  5790

Hydroponic Society of SA
c/- Bruce Retallick
12 Jikara Dve, Glen Osmond, 5064

Hydroponic Society of WA
c/- M. Biggs
Lot 13 Treeby Rd, Mandogalup,
  6167

Suppliers

Victoria

Sage Horticultural
121 Herald St, Cheltenham, 3192.
  Ph (03) 553 3777 (greenhouse,
  hydroponic and propagation
  supplies)

One Stop Sprinklers
645 Burwood Hwy, Vermont Sth,
  3133. Ph (03) 800 2177 or
  (057) 74 0665

Duralite Horticultural Supplies
54 Old Dandenong Rd,
  Heatherton, 3202. Ph (03)
  551 6756

Barnambirr Industries
Ph (03) 592 4298

Chemgro Industries
2 Glencourt St, Templestowe, 3106.
  Ph (03) 846 3401

Hydroponic City
cnr Dynon Rd & Radcliffe St,
  Kensington, 3031. Ph (03)
  376 0447

Hydroponic World (Eliza Bottoms
  Nursery)
27 Moorooduc Rd, Baxter, 3911.
  Ph (059) 71 1956

The Hydroponics Shop
270 Union Rd, Moonee Ponds,
  3039. Ph (03) 370 0402

Propine
160 Colchester Rd, Kilsyth, 3137.
  Ph (03) 728 2588, fax (03)
  728 1848 (media and fertilisers)

Axedale Sands & Gravels
PO Box 14, Axedale, 3551

Doug Willman
Old Murray Rd, Huntly, 3551

Growool
159 Wellington Rd, Clayton, 3168
  (rockwool)

Red Top Distributors
39 Horne St, Elsternwick, 3185.
  Ph (03) 528 4044 (vermiculite)

Greenlite Hydroponics
39 Burwood Hwy, Burwood, 3125.
  Ph (03) 888 8885 (hydroponic
  supplies, lights, nutrients, etc.)

Greenlantern Hydroponics
188 Warrigal Rd, Oakleigh, 3166.
  Ph (03) 563 7435 (Ted
  Garner—hydroponic supplies)

Toolangi Strawberry Runner
  Growers
Main Rd, Toolangi, 3777

Australian Hydroponics
410 Smith St, Collingwood, 3066.
  Ph (008) 335 980

Irelands Hydroponics &
  Horticultural Lighting
31 Main St, Kinglake, 3763.
  Ph (057) 86 1443

Lilydale Hydroponics
c/- PO, Lilydale, 3140

21st Century Products
176 Koornang Rd, Carnegie, 3163

Banksia Greenhouse Centre
Lot 26 Burwood Hwy, Burwood
  South, 3152

Magigro
31 Wilsons Rd, Doncaster, 3108
  (nutrients)

Phostrogen Australia
51 Princes St, Port Melbourne,
  3207 (nutrients)

Top Fertilisers P/L
25 Menton Place, Clayton, 3168

Mornington Hydroponics
12 Venice St, Mornington, 3931

Neuchatel
270 Hammond Rd, Dandenong,
  3175. Ph (03) 706 9898
  (vermiculite, perlite
  manufacturers)

Ausietrough
30 Shearson Cres., Mentone, 3194.
  Ph (03) 584 5622

New South Wales

Accent Hydroponics
87 Marigold St, Revesby, 2212.
  Ph (02) 772 3166

Soilless Cultivation Systems Aust.
  P/L
Box 119, Woollahra, 2025

Luwasa Hydroculture
18 Roseberry Rd, Kellyville, 2153.
  Ph (008) 025 651 (hydroponic
  planters)

R & D Aquaponics
12 Ferndell St, Granville, 2142

Simple Grow
Unit 28/132 Hassal St, Wetherill
  Park, 2164. Ph (02) 725 2150

Agrisorb P/L
45 Holt St, Surry Hills, 2010

Terra Temp P/L
6 Airds Rd, Minto, 2566

Flora Revolution
2 Grenfell St, Blakehurst, 2221

Leni Hydroculture
3 Chilcott Ave, Mt Hutton, 2290

Hydroyield Products
PO Box 508, Raymond Terrace,
  2324

Vinidex Tubemakers
PO Box 229 (15 Merriwa St),
  Gordon, 2072

Australian Perlite
20 McPherson St, Banksmeadow,
  2019

Bulk Hydroponic Nutrients
28/132 Hassal St, Wetherill Park,
  2164

Dural Irrigation
270 New Line Rd, Dural, 2158.
  Ph (02) 651 2760

Growool Horticultural Systems
2 Wiltona Pl, Girraween, 2145.
  Ph (02) 631 7007

Aira P/L
142 Beaconsfield St, Revesby, 2212

Airdraulic-Birco P/L
25 Dickson Ave, Artarmon, 2064

Air-temp-Raypak
11 Arkley St, Bankstown, 2200

Lighting Components P/L
20 Barry Ave, Mortdale, 2223.
  Ph (02) 570 7322

Australian Plastic Profiles P/L
2–10 Parraweena Rd, Taren Point,
  2229

Greenhouse Building Materials
69 Canterbury Rd, Canterbury,
  2193

Econo Greenhouse P/L
201 Darling St, Balmain, 2041

Commercial Glasshouses
39 Barry St, Kellyville, 2153

South Pacific Hydroponics
252 Oxford St, Bondi Junction,
  2022

Home Plant P/L
28/132 Hassall St, Wetherill Park,
  2164

Anne Palmer
3 Bond Close, Rankin Park, 2287

Top Fertilisers P/L
152 Magowar Rd, Girraween, 2145

R & D Chemicals
1 Park Rd, Rydalmere, 2116

The Garden Shelf
36 John Bull St, Queanbeyan,
  2620

Queensland

North Qld Hydroculture
PO Box 5597, MSO Townsville,
  4810

Hydroponic Industries
5 David St, Kenmore, 4096

Gold Coast Hydroponic Farm
Mt Tamborine Rd, Upper
  Coomera, 4210

Barmac Chemicals
14 Annie St, Rocklea, 4106.
  Ph (07) 277 3999

City Garden Hydroponics
1 Denham Tce, Tarragindi, 4121.

DJR Hydroponic Agencies
197 Duffield Rd, Kallangur, 4503.
  Ph (07) 204 4124

Grow Force Aust P/L
PO Box 88, Brisbane Market,
  4106

Australian Hydroponic Supply
  Centre
Cheshire Grove, Elanora, 4221.
  Ph (075) 33 9681

Sunnyclime Enterprises P/L
M/S 1020 Brisbane Valley Hwy,
Fernvale, 4305. Ph (075)
64 3842

Fensmore P/L
19 Hasp St, Seventeen Mile Rocks,
4073. Ph (07) 376 2744

Western Australia

Hydro and Garden Products
1 Belmont Rd, Kenwick, 6017

Fensmore Pty Ltd
20 King Edward Rd, Osborne
Parka, 6107

Hydrogarden Products
PO Box 335, Armadale, 6112

Hydroponics Aust. Pty Ltd
Birkdale St, Floreat, 6014

Aquaponics WA
Lot 12 Warton Rd, Canningvale,
6155. Ph (09) 455 2133

Growth Technology
244 South St, South Fremantle,
6162. Ph (09) 430 4713 (clonex,
nutrients, growth kits)

Perth Hydroponics Centre
270 Albany Hwy, Victoria Park,
6100. Ph (09) 361 8211

South Australia

Ace Chemical Co.
10 Wadonga St, Beverley, 5009

Fensmore Pty Ltd
1 Main Tce, Richmond, 5033
(hydroponic planters)

Adelaide and Wallaroo Fetlllsers
Francis St, Port Adelaide, 5015

Fengate Nursery
45 Wellington Rd, Mt Barker,
5251

Tasmania

Surges Bay Plant Farm
PO Box 27, Geeveston, 7116
(general nursery and
hydroponic supplies)

Overseas

Hydroponics Services Ltd
PO Box 4241, Mt Maunganui,
New Zealand

Auckland Hydroponic Centre Ltd
38 Georges Rd, Avondale,
Auckland, New Zealand

Aquaponics
22135 Ventura Bvde, Woodland
Hills, CA 91364, USA

Brady Manufacturing Co.
Box 134 RD4 Jackson, NJ, 08527,
USA

Cardinal Systems Inc.
Rt 61, RD1, Schuylkul Haven, PA,
17972, USA

Clover Garden Products
PO Box 874, VG7, Smyrna, TN,
37167, USA

Crop King
PO Box 310, Medina, OH 44258,
USA

Honeyacre Corp.
Suite 2, 21885 Highway 18, Apple
Valley, CA, 92307, USA

Hydro Division—Lear Siegler Inc.
375 Fifth Ave, New Brighton, MN
55112, USA

Hydrogardens Inc.
PO Box 9707, Colorado Springs,
CO 80932, USA

ICI Midox
Woolmead House West, Bear
Lane, Farnham, Surrey. GU9
7UB, UK

Ammerlaan Installaties
Noaldwijk, The Netherlands

B.V. Bastiaansen
Zanddereef 24, 4841 LD,
Prinsenbeek, The Netherlands

Grodania
Hovegaden 483, 2640
Medenhusene, Denmark

Hydroponic Farms

Booyong Hydroponic Farm
Ballina, NSW 2478
(lettuce/carnations)

F & I Bagley, Flower and Plant
Growers
Heatherton Rd, Clayton Sth, Vic.
3169

George Spriggs
Isaacs Rd, Pickering Brook, WA
6076

Ramco Farm
SA (strawberries)

170

References

Ball, G., Inc., Ball Red Book, *Greenhouse Growing*, Reston Publishing Co., Virginia, USA, 1985

Baxter, P. & Tankard, G., *Growing Fruit in Australia*, Nelson.

Bently, M., *Hydroponics Plus*, O'Connor Printers, South Dakota USA, 1974.

Burnley Horticultural College, *Commercial Applications of Hydroponics*, (seminar papers), Agriculture Note Series No. 12, May 1979.

Cooper, A., *The ABC of NFT*, Grower Books, London, 1979.

Dalton, L. & Smith, R., *Hydroponics Gardening*, Lothian, Melbourne, 1985.

Day, D., *Strawberries*, Grower Digest No. 3, Nov. 1988.

Douglas, J. S., *Beginners Guide to Hydroponics*, Pelham Books, London, 1984.

Douglas, J. S., *Advanced Guide to Hydroponics*, Pelham Books, 1989.

Grower Guide, *Cucumbers*, Grower Books, London, 1981.

Grower Magazine, Grower Publications, London.

Handreck, K. & Black, N., *Growing Media for Ornamental Plants and Turf*, New South Wales University Press, Sydney, 1984.

Harris, D. H., *Hydroponics*, Sphere Books Ltd, UK, 1977.

Hartley, M., *Rockwool in Horticulture:* seminar paper presented at the Summer Horticultural Update Seminar, Australian Horticultural Correspondence School, 1985.

Hartmann, H. T., Flocker, W. J. & Kofranek, A. M., *Plant Science: Growth, Development and Utilization of Cultivated Plants*, Prentice-Hall, USA, 1981.

Horst, R. K., *Westcott's Plant Disease Handbook*, Van Nostrand Reinhold, USA, 1979.

International Society on Soilless Culture. Conference proceedings (various).

Laurie, A., Kiplinger, D. C. & Nelson, K. S., *Commercial Flower Forcing*, McGraw-Hill, 1979.

Lorenz, O. A. & Maynard, D. N, *Knott's Handbook for Vegetable Growers*, John Wiley & Sons, New York, 1980.

Miller, R. A., *The Potential of Herbs as a Cash Crop*, Acres USA, 1985.

Nelson, P., *Greenhouse Operation and Management*, Prentice Hall, USA, 1985.

Resh, H. M., *Hydroponic Food Production*, Woolbridge Publishing Co., California, USA, 1989.

Reuter, D. J. & Robinson, J. B., *Plant Analysis: An Interpretation Manual*, Inkata Press, Melbourne, 1986.

Salinger, J. P., *Commercial Flower Growing*, Butterworths, New Zealand, 1985

Smith, D. L., *Peppers and Aubergines*, Grower Books, London, 1986.

Smith, D. L., *Rockwool in Horticulture*, Grower Books, London, 1986.

Stoughton, R. H., *Soilless Cultivation and Its Application to Commercial Hydropoics Crop Production*, United nations Food and Agriculture Organisation, Rome, 1969.

Sundstrom, A. C., *Simple Hydroponics for Australian and New Zealand Gardeners*, Viking O'Neill, Victoria, 1989.

Sutherland, S. K., *Hydroponics for Everyone*, Hyland House Publishing, Melbourne, 1986.

Tindall, H. D., *Commercial Vegetable Growing*, Oxford University Press, 1968.

Truog, E., *US Department of Agriculture Yearbook*, 1941–47, pp. 566–576.

Withers, B. & Vipond, S., *Irrigation: Design and Practice*, Batsford Academic, London, 1974.

Index